A SLOW BOAT TO PARIS

ANDREW BROCKIS

This book is dedicated to the spirit of adventure before dementia

Introduction

The traveller sees what he sees, the tourist sees what he has come to see

Gilbert K. Chesterton

Welcome to the tale of my travels through a France seldom visited by tourists. Travelling by boat is a special window-like opportunity that has enabled me to see into the lives of the real French people away from the well trodden path that most tourists take. As we meander erratically through the land peering voyeuristically over peoples back fences I am often granted different insights into what makes this country really tick.

Whilst I may often seem to mock the French, with their rigid adherence to a code of politeness that seems to defy comprehension, as well as both their total inability to grasp the concept of urgency, or pronounce the letter H, please don't misunderstand me, I love this country and its joyous idiosyncrasies.

Many times the frustrating delays that occurred in France acted like a mirror showing me how obsessed most of us have become with the instant gratification that seems so important in most countries today. Instant email, mobile phones, and instant coffee, why wait? We live in a world that wants everything NOW. Faced with inevitable Gallic delays that pass for normality in the hexagon of France, I have now learned to say *merde*, and shrug my shoulders in recognition of the inevitable. If I have to wait for something, I have found that it really doesn't matter *c'est la vie*. This is something most French people seem to understand organically.

We had many guests visit us aboard during our travels. Whilst I can honestly say we enjoyed them all, it was interesting getting an insight into the lives of our friends as well as those of foreigners. If you can smile at someone who has just blocked your toilet and blown up your power supply and then pretend it is not important you must be good friends indeed.

As usual some names have been changed due to complete cowardice on my part, specifically to avoid any aggrieved parties sending a large bloke called Hugo or Brutus around to feed me a knuckle sandwich. Besides, guilty parties, you know who you are anyway.

To my friends who took part in this adventure, but most of all to my long suffering wife Trish without whom neither the cruise nor this book could have happened, I thank you.

I am writing this foreword looking out of my boat cabin window, and the water of the canal is like a mirror outside. It is eight o'clock in the evening and the sun has yet to set on the little village of St. Léger sur Dheune. Small fish surface nearby as if to wish me *bonsoir*. The old stone houses on the bank, with their peeling paint and shuttered windows are whispering stories. It is so beautiful that a tear rolls down my cheek, I wish you could be here to share the experience of France.

Andrew Brockis
St. Léger sur Dheune.
France 2013

You only live once, but if you do it right, once is enough

Mae West

The telephone rang so insistently that resisting its cacophony would be useless. Reluctantly, I raised my head from the pillow in the dark and fumbled about on the bedside table until I found the receiver and lifted it to my ear.

"G'day Andy, did'ya know there's a bloody big hole in the back of our boat mate?" My best friend Trevor's amplified voice crackled down the phone line startling me awake like vat of hot Java. I sat on the edge of my bed in a Paris hotel room the size of a broom closet and struggled to get my brain to grasp what he was saying.

"A hole in our new boat," how is that even possible? " I blurted in reply.

That morning Trevor had arrived at a small marina in Castelnaudary, a provincial town in the south of France and he appeared to be referring to a boat that we had bought to pursue our dream of cruising from the Mediterranean to Paris.

His words bounced around my sleep starved brain like ping pong balls in a blender, as I struggled to understand what he was trying to tell me. Whatever it was it didn't sound good, as he proceeded to explain that the condition of our new bateau purchased sight

6

unseen on the internet, had massively underwhelmed him. As he continued to list a litany of problems with the boat, I looked out the window at the sleeting rain falling on the Place de la Bastille. Outside the weather was as damp and miserable as the news flooding down the telephone line.

So much for sunny springtime Paris and canal cruising in glorious sunshine, I thought to myself as I reached for my dressing gown to ward off the morning chill that made my closet sized hotel room feel like a refrigerator. "I'm off to my hotel now to consider our options and cushion the blow with a large therapeutic whisky," said Trevor, snapping me back to the matter in hand. The phone clicked in my ear severing our connection and going straight back to bed for a big sulk looked very attractive, after all there are some days one should just admit defeat and stay there and this was definitely shaping up to be one of those days.

It was not the first time Trevor and I had bought a boat together and our history of shared vessels had not so far been a good one. As university students, we once bought an old wooden launch that had been languishing on the dock for years innumerable, doing a convincing impersonation of firewood. We thought it would make the perfect party boat and be a chick magnet guaranteed to attract every well filled bikini on campus. We spent a long hot summer on sweltering concrete hard-standing, renovating, plugging holes and finally painting her a rather festive red, white and blue that drew raised eyebrows from the conservative senior members of the yacht club.

After several months of this unaccustomed manual labour, we were eventually ready to set sail and let the good times roll. Anxious to get the party started, we pooled our meagre savings and hired a mobile crane to launch the boat back into the water. We were ready to embark on the sort of voyages of nautical depravity that would have made Blackbeard blush. True, we still had

7

no motor, but surely that wouldn't deter the bikini clad ladies who would enthusiastically flock to our floating sin palace.

On the great day of the launch our loyal friends gathered at the yacht club to admire the giant crane which raised the boat from its cradle and then ceremoniously lowered it gently to kiss the surface of the water for the first time in years. However, as the crane kept lowering her down, the party boat floated with all the lightness and grace of a bowling ball. It didn't even have the goodness to flounder about on the surface, but instead just sank straight to the muddy bottom of the river. Champagne from the christening bottles dribbled disconsolately onto the dock, as we all froze in shock and stood horrified watching, not knowing what to say about the embarrassing debacle unfolding in front of us.

"Don't worry mate, she'll be right. The dry timbers of a planked hull are gonna take time to re-hydrate. You gotta expect a bit of seepage at first." proffered one old salt who happened to be passing.

It was a small consolation, but this wasn't just seepage, on a scale of one to ten it was an eleven, a regular Niagara Falls. Sill as a submarine, our ship was a total success.

The embarrassed crowd of well-wishers packed up their champagne and rapidly evaporated, muttering things like "Titanic" and "Epic cock-up". We picked up our shattered pride and shuffled off home leaving the submerged boat to soak, take up water and hopefully seal the leaks.

During the month that followed, we returned to the hulk now known as That Bloody Boat, each week and dutifully baled her out hoping for some improvement. Each time as we pumped frantically, she would rise up from the depths, wallow a bit and then go straight back down as soon as we stopped pumping.

Eventually, after several months of continued failure to seal the hull, the long-suffering yacht club lost patience with the ugly shipwreck on their doorstep and cast us adrift, telling us in no uncertain terms to move her elsewhere.

Lacking the cash to hire another crane, or even a motorised pump we co-opted a crew of students, who fortified by generous quantities of beer, baled heroically and managed to keep the wreck afloat long enough for us to tow it upriver, where it sank and lay ignominiously rotting on a piece of vacant shoreline like the wreck of the Hesperus.

Months passed and our subsequent attempts to salvage That Bloody Boat continued without success, thus it wasn't a big surprise to receive a threatening letter from the local Marine and Harbours Office.

Bugger! The bastards now knew where I lived. The grand Admiral in charge of the Swan River office wrote in legal jargon dripping with venom, that our beached wreck was creating a sandbar and was considered a hazard to navigation. His missive was accompanied by threats of great financial impoverishment for me. Unfortunately, the bureaucrats were not impressed with my reply, in which I generously offered to plant a couple of palm trees on the wreck and suggested that they consider charting it as a new island.

Over the following weeks the official letters continued and the accompanying threats increasing in ferocity each time. Eventually, cowed by fear of the establishment, but with no cash left for another rescue, it was time for desperate measures.

Early one Saturday just before daybreak, I crept down to the swamped hulk armed with two large jerry cans of petrol. After checking that no one was about to witness my deeds, I doused the boat with the the whole 40 litres. Next I ran a trail of gas along the beach and from a respectable distance I tossed on a match and ran. The resulting explosion and apocalyptic flames were impressive to behold and created a column of oily black smoke, which filled the morning sky like the aftermath of a dirty big Atom bomb.

From my vantage point concealed behind a bush, I waited for the inevitable crowds of spectators, constabulary, fire brigade and the media to arrive with sirens blaring to investigate the great conflagration. Imagine my disappointment when nobody took the slightest notice of the pyrotechnic extravaganza? Did people let off massive Molotov cocktails every morning in this neighbourhood ? If I tried that stunt today, I would be banged up by the local SWAT team, dressed in an orange jump suit and sent off for a Guantanamo style interview conducted by a large person waving a rubber hose pipe.

But this was the seventies, so for ten minutes I watched alone as flames shot dramatically skywards and finally when the holocaust had subsided and still nobody had showed up, I emerged from my hiding place to admire my handiwork.

I couldn't believe the result, That Bloody Boat was still intact, it had refused to die. The paintwork was hardly singed and though the red and blue paint job now looked a depressing shade of sepia it looked like the whole damn thing was indestructible.

The sorry tale of the BB ended happily for me a few weeks later, when somebody pinched what remained of the carcass and that was the last we ever heard of it. For years I cherished a secret dream that someone had renovated her and that I would one day discover her restored and reclaim her. So far no luck, but I keep looking.

Back in reality, forty years later, here were Trevor and I in France, on a second attempt at boat ownership and it was with apparent déja vu not starting well. Had we bought another floating turkey?

What had possessed us to come to the other side of the world and buy another old boat without even seeing it first? Was it the romantic idea of living in a foreign country unable to talk to anyone, or to understand their media, like linguistic castaways on a desert island of French?

A psychologist could write a long and very boring thesis, about what drives a couple of middle aged blokes to leave their comfy suburban ruts, to live on the other side of the world in a small leaky box with primitive plumbing and its own ecosystem of mildew. But who cares? I'm not a big believer in the self-absorptive analysis of people who spend their days looking up their own backsides. I reckon Psychology, is the study of people who don't need studying, by people who do. Nevertheless there had to be a reason why we were doing this.

Perhaps my Francophilic cravings were genetic? My father spent a lot of his final years researching our family tree. At the time I wondered what he was hoping to find, perhaps a branch bearing a neglected inheritance, or a twig with a distant link to the throne? After many years of fossicking through old English church records and graveyards, in the end all he discovered were tales of defrocked vicars and other ne'er do wells. Until finally one day his persistence paid off when dear old Dad discovered that we are descendants of the French knight Sir Bernard Brocas a resident of the English court.

Unfortunately, the good Sir Bernard came to a sticky end when he picked the wrong side in a failed royal coup d'état and King Henry IV beheaded him in 1400. In a twist of fate realising later that he had been a bit hasty pruning the son of one of his best chums and keen to make up for his gaffe, King Hank ordered a Brocas family tomb built in Westminster Abbey where it can still be seen today. Did this mean that my English blood was mixed with the onion and garlic of Gascony? Was this drawing me to France, was it hereditary calling?

I think that the real epiphany that finally drop kicked me over the start line of leaving the rat race, came from an old patient of mine a Catholic priest, Father Brian.

One day as I sat in my dental emporium waiting for the local anaesthetic I had just administered to kick in, I started banging on about life, the universe and other *merde* with Father B.

'I have a gig at eleven o'clock' he said through a numb lip that was starting to look like it might slide off the side of his head, as he worriedly looked at his watch.

"What kind of gig could you possibly have on a Tuesday morning, some clandestine Catholic ritual perhaps?" I asked intrigued, my thoughts channelling the Da Vinci Code

 "A funeral service mate, and whilst it won't make any difference to the star of the show if I show up a bit late, the living can get a bit peeved if they're kept waiting for a good send-off" His face which had now slumped from the effect of the Novocaine made his words slur but he persevered with an answer.

'Talking of funerals, of all the people I have given the last rights, not one ever said; "If only I'd spent more time at the office,' Makes you think that, doesn't it?'

Indeed it did make me think, his sage advice had hit a nerve, coming at a time when undiagnosed ailments were starting to take a toll of my ageing peers. Some were having exotic bits of stainless steel carpentered into their backs and knees, others lengths of tubing stuffed into their arteries and veins. One bloke never left home without a generous supply of blue Viagra pills and a pharmacopoeia capable of medicating a third world country for a month. A few others had even fallen unexpectedly off their perches and gone to the great tax haven in the sky. (I am sure heaven was just a biblical spelling mistake).

I remember that my father once told me that he had experienced a period between age sixty and seventy years, when he lost a few old mates and he said that he felt like a season ticket holder at the local cemetery.

"Nature had a bit of a sorting out process amongst my friends and colleagues at that time. I started to check the funeral notices in the paper each morning to see if I was listed and the whole thing got a bit depressing," said Dad.

Was this to be my future too, checking the broadsheets for signs of life? Was this all there was between now and the great goodnight, more life in the dental surgery, gum gardening and plugging fangs?

Determined not to shuffle off the mortal coil with a bucket list of unfinished fun, I decided it was time to flee the office and began to plan my escape from suburbia.

My new motto would be Adventure before Dementia. I would sell my dental practice, buy a boat and sail around the world. It all sounded so easy, but there was just one problem, my wife Trish.

Trish has put up with me for over forty years and I am very attached to her, but she is not a natural sailor and she made it very clear that deep blue oceans and seasickness held no appeal for her. She had no desire to see her breakfast more than once a day.

"You're on your own there dear, I'll fly ahead and wait for you on a tropical beach well supplied with masseurs and comfort," she offered as a compromise. Sleep deprived, lonely and terrifying solo sailing was not really the life on the ocean wave that I had dreamed of and so my blue water dream was doomed before it started.

With that fantasy shattered, each day as I toiled over a smoking drill, the walls of my office seemed to be closing in on me, until one day a conversation about the future turned back to holidays we had spent on the French inland waterways. Leisurely trips on the Canal du Midi and through the Alsace Lorraine, where there were no storms, or dragging anchors, no navigational challenges, nor customs hassles, just good food, sun and wine.

"Maybe the French canals could be the answer. Why don't we buy a canal boat there?" suggested Trish bless her heart.

The more we discussed the idea, the better it looked. The plan was simple like my brother in law George. But unlike George this would work. We could have the best of both worlds, I would get to live on a boat and Trish wouldn't have to deal with seasickness or the perils of the ocean.

So was born our plan to buy a boat and cruise the length and breadth of France from the Mediterranean to the centre of Paris.

A few days later well lubricated by a delicious bottle of Châteauneuf du Pape we shared our idea over dinner with our good friends Trevor and Jenny who took one look at each other and insisted on having a slice of the action and a boating partnership was reborn.

What followed next was months spent researching magazines, books and Googling questions like; How does one buy a boat in a France? What would be best, a wood, fibre glass or steel hull? What about the paper work, and permits required? The more we looked the more t practicalities came into question.

Many answers came to us when we discovered a charter boat company, that had been hit by the global financial crisis. With global tourism at an all time low, they were rationalising their fleet by selling off their older boats and had flooded the market with twenty ex rental boats of varying sizes, ages and condition all at fire sale prices. It was a buyer's smorgasbord and the perfect timing for us meant we were ready to pounce on a bargain like a dingo in a chook house.

We began negotiating with the charter company's broker Monsieur Molyneux and received by email a detailed set of pictures of a suitable boat and also a plan of the its interior layout.

It was forty-six feet long in old money units and although it wasn't a traditional style of barge like a péniche, its stylish modern look appealed to us, as did its three double cabins, a cabin with two bunks, a dinette study, and a large living area/kitchen. Not to forget the three bathrooms that meant at least we would be the cleanest mariners afloat if not the best dressed. To rag and string yachtsmen like us who were used to the confined quarter-berth squalor and narrow companionways of sailboats, it looked to us like a floating Taj Mahal.

Our previous experience with That Bloody Boat, meant that we knew only too well the infinite number of faults and flaws that a vessel can hide. To avoid these pitfalls we decided to call in an expert to survey our boat before buying it. Well, that was indeed the plan, but our attempts to engage an independent surveyor were thwarted by the boat's inland location. All French marine surveyors are located near the coast and none was either available or willing to travel inland without the minimum promise of a briefcase of Euros, Rolls Royce transport, five star accommodation and an interesting love affair as a sweetener. This was all a bit out of our price bracket, as we had been thinking more of a second class rail ticket, a backpackers dorm and a manly handshake to seal the deal.

Not surprisingly, we were unable to obtain a reasonably priced survey and as our arrival date in France approached, we were faced with the very likely prospect of having nowhere to live if the boat was sold to another party. In a fit of panic, we agreed to take a risk, forgo the survey and buy the boat unseen. This might turn out to be a mistake, but how bad could it be? We would find out.

It transpired that the purchase transaction was a wonderfully French experience. After corresponding about a boat unimaginatively named Challenger Two, for a couple of months and having received a full inventory and portfolio of photographs, we made an offer to buy.

Next day we received a prompt reply by email that our offer had been enthusiastically accepted. However, footnote to the letter pointed out that we could not actually have the boat we had been negotiating for, as it had been sold from under us, instead we could have an entirely different vessel Challenger One. We were assured it was the same and that there would be no problems with this surrogate. As they say in Thailand, "Same same ....but different".

In for a centime in for a Euro and somewhat desperate, we agreed to the substitution the money changed hands and Challenger One was ours.

But this was all in the past, now it was April, we were in France and I was hearing that the description "No problems," apparently included an iceberg sized hole in the stern of our new home.

Bugger!

Keen to get to grips with the boat and see the situation for ourselves Trish and I caught the first available train from the Gare de Lyon in Paris to Toulouse.

I love the way French trains run on time and I especially enjoy the five-note SNCF railway jingle that precedes every platform announcement. I call it the 'Happy Song', because it somehow exemplifies French travel to me. It's a musical statement that seems to say, "There is a train going somewhere soon if you feel like getting aboard, but if you don't, *pas de problème* there is no hurry and life is too beautiful to rush. Besides there will always be another one *n'est ce pas* so I will play the Happy song again for you soon.

Trish has had to drag me off railway platforms more than once, when I stood mesmerised by that jingle as it played over the public address system for every departing or arriving train.

16

Once aboard, the TGV shot us south across France at neck snapping speed though the countryside was hidden from our view as it flashed by by a veil of drizzling rain. It felt like no time at all until we arrived at our destination i Toulouse.

It was grey and wet in Toulouse that evening as Trish and I stepped onto the platform. With our bags in tow we exited the station and walked through a cluster of a dozen, dreadlocked gypsies in their uniforms of congealed grubby black denim. They were Romanies, congregated in the shelter at the front of the old railway terminal each accompanied by a huge menacing black dog. Forty years ago they would have been hippies in rainbow coloured finery radiating peace and love and a haze of organic wacky tobaccy. Nowadays in France nomadic travellers are merely an ugly stain on the landscape of big city cathedrals and railway stations, to which they cling like a bad smell, alternately begging, or just looking malevolent.

One of the gypsy girls half heartedly tried the old scam of pretending to have found a ring that she thrust at me insisting it was mine. As soon as the mark takes the proffered ring it is followed by demands for payment that become progressively more threatening. Having encountered this con before, I put the ring on the ground and walked away from it, much to her vociferously feigned disgust. This de facto welcome to Toulouse did nothing to lighten our already somber mood and I couldn't help but feel that her presence was denying a village somewhere of its idiot.

We trudged off towards a nearby hotel, checked in and found ourselves allocated a very compact room for the night. There wasn't enough space to swing an emaciated cat and the bathroom was literally a converted wardrobe which required advanced yoga contortions to enter.

When the post-war tourism boom struck France, to capitalise on the influx of visitors every linen closet was converted into a hotel room. This left the Frogs with an appalling lack of storage space for sheets and pillow cases.

'Ah but Pierre where will I store ze sheets?'

'No problem Maman, hang zem out the windows like flags." And thus was born the national pastime of airing bed linen out the *fenêtres* and flying the brave white flags which have featured so prominently in French military history.

By now it was getting late in Toulouse and our stomachs were rumbling demandingly, so before retiring to our closet for the night, we walked to the inauspicious looking restaurant we had spotted earlier near the railway station. By now the gypsies had closed up shop for the night or been moved on by the Gendarmerie, improving the scenery but the grimy facade and dirty windows of the station restaurant did little to inspire confidence in its cuisine. Nevertheless, it was the only place open at this time of night, so we took our appetites inside and hoped for the best.

It was brilliant. Straight out of the nineteen forties, the décor was like the café of the sixties TV show 'Allo Allo'. It was a classic, right down to blackened bent wood chairs, ornate nicotine stained ceiling and an atmosphere that had us expecting Monsieur René and the Resistance to walk in at any moment. The food when it arrived was also excellent and we both enjoyed a delicious duck confit. That was one duck that did not die in vain, it was full of flavour and just melted away in the mouth.

The classic recipe for confit is to fry or grill duck legs in a bucket of duck fat until they are well-browned and crisp. Then use more of the fat to roast some potatoes and garlic as an accompaniment. Every mouthful is guaranteed to send the cholesterol meter right off the scale. After fortifying ourselves with a bottle of grease stripping vin rouge we felt that the world had taken a turn for the better and expressing our appreciation to the chef, we returned to the hotel and squeezed into our cupboard for the night.

Next morning the rain had cleared and the sun was pushing its way through the overcast, creating patches of beautiful blue sky and a hope that today might somehow be brighter than its predecessor.

Downstairs in the breakfast room, resplendent with peeling *fleur de lys* wallpaper, and worn floorboards, we enjoyed a petit déjeuner of coffee and croissants and had no sooner finished eating than Trevor arrived in his hire car to pick us up and ferry us to the boat in Castelnaudary.

He was dressed in his customary uniform of baggy hibiscus board shorts and singlet. Trevor's sartorial splendour is worn rain or shine from Broome to London and is occasionally garnished with an old school tie on formal occasions. Trevor is a solid bloke, with short curly dark hair on top of a jovial face that houses a smile so warm you could toast cheese on it. Trevor was accompanied by his long suffering wife Jenny, who long ago abandoned any attempt to rein in his fashion tastes and now just good naturedly shrugs as if to say, "Well what can I do?'.

After the emotional blow yesterday of discovering the boat to be in such poor shape, Trevor's good humour had returned and this morning he was radiating his usual hundred-kilowatt smile and infectious *bonheur*. Influenced by his effervescence and the very welcome morning sunshine, everything today seemed more positive and once our luggage was loaded into the compact rental car we all squeezed aboard for the short drive to Castelnaudary.

Historically Castelnaudary is famous for two things. During a siege in the war of One Hundred Years (1337-1453), it is said that the famous bean dish, Cassoulet, was first invented there.

With the town surrounded by an English army, food supplies were running dangerously low, the soldiers were weakening and the defenders couldn't hope to hold out much longer. The beleaguered townsfolk brought together all the remaining supplies of beans, vegetables, pigs and poultry, from which the city cooks prepared a single dish, a great '*cassole*.' It was a hearty dish served out to restore strength to the brave defenders and thus the Cassoulet was born. After the fortifying meal was washed down with a few vineyards of wine, the Chaurienne, as the inhabitants of Castelnaudary are known, fell upon the encircling English army, who not supplied with such gourmet cooking immediately panicked. The locals then raised the siege and chased away their enemies who according to legend did not stop running, until they reached the shores of the Channel.

In a footnote to the rout of the unfortunate English army, it should be noted that if the beans in a Cassoulet are not pre-soaked before cooking, they produce a lot of gas and the consumer will swell up like a Zeppelin, before emitting large volumes of strong beanie fumes that reek of rotting dinosaur. This resultant flatulence amongst the French army may indeed have been the first undocumented use of gas warfare, and perhaps explains why the numerically superior Pommy army legged it so fast.

A Cassoulet is served in a glazed ceramic dish full of white beans with a thick slice of free-range Gascon pork, delicious sausage and a big piece of duck confit, it is a culinary masterpiece. For such a hearty dish, the taste is surprisingly delicate, with whiffs of thyme and garlic, and each meat holds its own in a dense broth. Castelnaudary remains famous for Cassoulet today and the dish is celebrated each year during the last week of August at the Festival of the Cassoulet. It is available in most local restaurants, as well as being exported from several factories that comprise the main industry of the town.

A second historical event and one of greater importance to our nautical venture occurred during 1668, when an artificial lake known as Le Grand Bassin, was created below the town centre as part of the new canal scheme. A big inland port was built, which added much to the town's commerce and importance in the region and it was here that we would find Challenger One waiting for us. Today the commercial canal traffic is long gone, but the place retains it's own particular charm.

On the edge of town is a base of la Légion Etrangère, The Foreign Legion, are a very sensible military solution to the French reluctance of being shot at, in which the Republic hires a bunch of cannon fodder mercenaries to fight their wars for them. This very practical idea and the legendary bravery of the legionnaires with their heroic 'Never surrender,' motto has lead to the closing of several white flag factories across France. But there will be more about the legion later.

From the quayside of the Bassin, where dedicated fishermen sit camped all night, with multiple fishing rods set up on stands, hoping to catch the giant fish that live there, to the busy central market square that forms the beating heart of the town, we would come to feel very at home in Castelnaudary.

It was noon when we arrived at the port. The sun was still shining and the sleepy little town was closed for the midi lunch break. As we pulled into the marina, there she was, we saw our boat suspended precariously in a crane sling on the quayside.

Since Trevor's initial inspection, the maintenance crew been hard at work, they had repaired the stern of the boat and painted the hull with a fresh coat of glistening white enamel, so there was no remaining sign of the catastrophic hole. All in all Challenger One our new home now looked pretty good.

'Wow, she looks a lot better than yesterday,' confirmed Trevor, plainly reassured that perhaps there might be hope after all and that we might not need to break out the jerry cans of petrol after all this time .

"Let's take a look inside, they wouldn't let me aboard yesterday until the supporting props had been checked."

As if on cue, Monsieur Molyneux the broker responsible for both the sale as well as the unconventional switch of boats, returned from lunch. A tall handsome young man with a relaxed manner, Frédèric produced both a key and a ladder and we took the opportunity to climb aboard and examine our new home.

It looked awesome. The varnished wood paneling of the forward and aft cabins felt warm and inviting. The spaciousness of the saloon/kitchen area amidships with its 360 degree panoramic windows, through which we would enjoy the scenery as we floated towards gay Paree, was just what we had hoped for. This boat even had a working engine, so there would be no stopping us now. Everything seemed to be in good shape, so we signed the handover papers and Challenger One was ours.

That afternoon the marina crew lowered her back into the water. Unlike her predecessor, she floated nicely on the surface. The yard crew moved her to a vacant space and tied her stern to their wharf and we wasted no time in moving aboard.

That night we cooked a celebration dinner that was washed down with a lake of vin rouge and contentedly poured ourselves into our beds to dream of the carefree days that lay ahead.

If only we had known what fate had in store for us, we might not have slept so soundly!

Castelnaudary Cassoulet

140g pork rind
140g smoked streaky bacon
300g Toulouse sausages
600g dried haricot beans, soaked
overnight in 3 times their volume of water
1 celery stick
1 small onion , preferably a white skinned mild
one
1 large carrot
6 garlic cloves
25g goose fat or 2 tbsp olive oil
1 bouquet garni
8 pinches of sea salt
2 pinches of freshly ground black pepper
1 clove , lightly crushed
2 tsp lemon juice

TO FINISH
4 confit duck legs
60g goose fat or 2 tbsp olive oil
40g dried breadcrumbs
1 garlic clove, finely chopped
a handful of fresh flat leaf parsley, coarsely
chopped

1.To cut the meats, roll up the pork rind like a
Swiss roll. With the seam underneath, use a
very sharp knife to cut the roll across into thin
slices, then chop the rolled-up slices across
into dice. Chop the bacon into small cubes
(lardons). Cut the garlic sausage into 1cm thick
slices.

2.Drain the soaked beans and discard the
soaking water. Tip the beans into a large
saucepan, add the diced pork rind and lardons

and cover with fresh cold water. Bring to the boil and blanch for 15-20 minutes.

3.Drain the beans, rind and lardons into a colander, and discard the cooking water.
Roughly chop the celery, onion and carrot. Peel the garlic cloves but leave them whole. Preheat the oven to 120C/fan 100C.

4.Heat the goose fat or olive oil in a 26cm flameproof casserole or deep overproof sauté pan over a low heat and sweat the celery, onion, carrot and garlic for 5 minutes. Add the bouquet garni and cook slowly to get a sugary caramelisation (about 5 minutes). Add the sausage, beans, pork rind and lardons and pour in 1.2 litres/2 pints water. Bring to the boil, skim off the scum, then add the salt, pepper, clove and lemon juice.

5.Transfer the casserole to the oven and cook, uncovered, for 2 hours, stirring every hour. At the end of this time, the beans will be soft and creamy in texture and the juices should have thickened. You may need to cook it for longer than 2 hours (say up to 2½ hours) to get to this stage - it depends

6.Remove the cassoulet from the oven. Bury the duck legs in the beans and sprinkle over the goose fat or olive oil, breadcrumbs and garlic. Return to the oven and cook for a further 2 hours. Serve the cassoulet in bowls, sprinkled with chopped parsley.

Welcome Aboard

It was our second night aboard, and the rain had returned with a vengeance. A veritable deluge was pouring down as I lay in my bunk dreaming of Noah's Ark and the perils of flooding, when I was awoken by water dripping onto my head. It trickled down my nose and soaked into my pillow, which rapidly became a sodden lump underneath me. As the first grey light of dawn oozed through the window, I struggled to remember where I was and I tried to make a case for starting the day. Staying bed sounded far more attractive, though I soon rejected the idea outright as a bad plan, as the incessant dripping of the water persisted meant that there was nothing for it but to shake myself and get up.

So there I was lying in a cold wet bunk not only was the rain pelting down outside the boat, but worse still, it was now raining inside as well. The dawn seeped into the cabin had revealed pools of water everywhere, as rain continued to trickle in from leaks throughout the boat. The roof was doing a good imitation of a tea strainer so Jenny and Trish commandeered every water-container they could find to place under the cascade that was flooding in from the leaking windows. Water was even coming down through the ceiling. It was as if every seam in the boat was opening at once.

"We'll have to plug the holes mate," cried Trevor, as he shot out the main hatch still resplendent in his baggy hibiscus shorts and nothing else. This was a sight no-one should be exposed to first thing in the morning, but inspired by his exuberance or panic (It was hard to tell which it was,) I joined him on deck and together we desperately tried to seal the window joints with duct tape.

Of course duct tape doesn't stick to wet surfaces, so all we succeeded in doing was tying each other up in black sticky knots and losing large painful clumps of leg and chest hair.

After twenty minutes of miserable failure, we retreated to the cabin, to find that the girls had things almost under control. Though the rain was still coming in, there were now pots, pans, tea cups and saucers scattered around the floors and tables to contain the drips and we could see that we were no longer in imminent danger of sinking.

I went back to my wet bed, pulled the rug over my head and tried to get some sleep, but it was no good, my duvet was a swollen sponge and the mattress was completely saturated. There was nothing for it, this was going to mean a morning spent at a Laundromat drying everything out, so after a breakfast of soggy Corn Flakes and limp baguette, we packed our sheets, covers and pillows into several enormous garbage bags which were strapped to the back of the bikes and the girls set off to the Laundromat. As they pedalled away I could hear them cursing ominously about boats and the male fools who loved them.

Meanwhile, reinforced by caffeine, Trevor and I fearing a feminist mutiny, decided that there was but one thing to do, we would have to remove and reseal all the windows and we set to work detaching the offending panes from their frames. After several hours of alternating scraping with swearing and stripping skin off our fingers, we had re-installed the worst windows with new silicone seals when it started to rain again.

That night we were able to reduce the number of pots and pans in service, but the boat still leaked and in the morning more sodden bedding meant it was back to the *laverie* for the girls, a process that was likely to be repeated for the foreseeable future or until the rain let up.

At the local washhouse, Trish and Jenny were now considered regulars and received a warm welcome from Monsieur Pierrot owner, whose retirement plans were being well subsidised daily by these saturated Antipodeans.

During the next few days into the gaps we pumped enough silicone to enhance the entire cast of the Folies Bergère but we slowly gained ground on the leaks. With less rain getting in, the interior dried out and at last we could take stock of the extent of the water damage.

There was a strong musty smell in the aft cabin and when we removed the wall panel, we discovered a penicillin factory of black mould that looked like an alien life form rapidly replicating and threatening to take over the boat. It was the sort of fungus you couldn't beat to death with a stick and it took some trench warfare strength chlorine, which set our heads spinning, as well as lots of elbow grease to finally shift it.

A week later during which time the sun came out only rarely, we conquered, the last of the rain leaks and made good progress with the other repairs that are were to be expected on an old boat. At last able to turn our attention to getting underway.

We had arrived in France believing that our Australian Skippers licenses would be recognised, but as soon as we enquired locally it became obvious that this was not actually the case.

"Monsieur your boat is registered in France, so you must have a French license to drive it on the French waterways *naturellement*!" said the all-powerful man at the waterways office of the Voies Nationale de France (VNF) when we made our enquiry.

The reality now dawned on us that without skippers permits we were effectively marooned in

Castelnaudary, unable to leave the dock without invalidating our insurance.

Fortunately, the purchase agreement included free mooring at the marina and this proved to be a godsend. We decided that until we could sort out the skippers tickets, we would set to completing our boat repairs with renewed vigour.

The marina staff seemed mildly embarrassed about the condition of the boat they had sold us, so they were extremely generous with their help and advice. Cans of fibreglass resin, bits of wood, or spare fenders would mysteriously appear out of their warehouse and be left next to our boat in the evenings, to aid our repairs for the following day.

Two weeks passed smoothly until one day we realised that we had fallen into a comfortable routine. Mornings were spent working on the boat, before adjourning to our favourite café in the town square for coffee and the local newspaper. Then of course it was midi and everyone including us stopped for lunch. Afternoons were spent planning and shopping for the wonderful dinners that would in the evening emerge from our well equipped galley and of course time had to be spent confusing the natives with our well intentioned, but clumsy attempts at speaking French.

Language problems had so far meant we had completely failed to open a local bank account, something we were really beginning to feel would be essential to our travels.

The French banking has some rather punitive rules for issuers of bad cheques. Offenders are banned from financial transactions for five years if they fail to pay their debts. All banks in the country receive real-time information on bad-cheque writers. Such people still face jail terms if they do it a second time.

The French system doesn't recognise many common credit cards such as Mastercard unless issued through the European Maestro system and also works on a debit only basis. If you haven't got money in the bank you can't spend it. Good sense really, but it does mean that most foreign cards won't work on everyday machines like petrol pumps and the ticket dispensers at railway stations. So we really needed a French bank account.

Unfortunately, every time we had tried to negotiate opening an account the seemingly insurmountable problem of not having a French postal address reared up. Post 9/11 and the Global Financial Crisis, banks were reluctant to do business with geriatric gypsies who communicated in Franglais and lived on a boat of no fixed address.

Then one day Trevor stumbled into the last bank in Castelnaudary left to try and he discovered Emily. Ahhh! Emily, the gorgeous branch manager for a local bank, that contained two people, a cat and enough entrance security to defeat a heavily armed siege. The delectable Emily was born of French father and English mother and spoke fluent English as well as her native French. Imagine Angelina Jolie with a bit of Nigella Lawson, then add a seductive French accent and you will understand why Trevor and I developed an instant passion for French banking. In future no transaction would be too small to necessitate a personal visit to see Mademoiselle Emily.

With the language barrier at the bank now overcome, Emily immediately sorted our no fixed address problem by imaginatively using the bank's own address and we became the proud owners of French bank accounts. Voila! With a French bank account now we could get a mobile phone. With a mobile phone account we could arrange Internet access and so the domino cascade of goodness rolled on.

Before long a month had passed. Although now ship shape and watertight, we were still uncertain what bureaucratic peril might befall us if we defied the rules and cruised illegally without skippers tickets.   Whilst

29

laissez faire, is a very tolerant attitude and many French laws and rules are often disregarded as mere 'suggestions,' we had been warned that if the proper permits were not in place and we had an accident, then all the fire of officialdom might rain down on us. We were too chicken to want to see the inside of a French chokey and we deemed it prudent not to leave the dock until we could obtain proper papers.

During that month our French language comprehension had started to improve. At first we were all a bit nervous to even open our mouths, so conversation was limited to '*Bonjour Madame*' and '*Il pleut aujourd'hui,*' which was always a safe bet as the rain persisted most days almost without pause.

We had all made some amusing blunders as we struggled to make ourselves understood. In the bricolage, I told the hardware store assistant that I would 'Roll over yesterday,' when I really meant 'I will return tomorrow.' I didn't realise why she looked so amused, until I got home and checked the dictionary.

We also adapted to the French *paysan* way of doing business. Like country folk everywhere things move at a more relaxed pace in a rural setting. This can be very frustrating for city dwellers used to instant gratification, until one accepts that deadlines are not a high priority here and that no amount of urgent bluster will make any difference. In fact it is likely to be interpreted very negatively by the natives and bring the wheels of progress to a complete stop.

"Today", means it 'may' happen today or perhaps tomorrow, or maybe the next day, because French time is very elastic. There was no point raising ones blood pressure trying to expedite matters. A simple order of new boat batteries, which would be same day delivery at home, took nine days, but there was no use fretting about delays, the locals were not to be hurried and that was that. So of necessity we learned to become more *tranquille.*

One morning whilst perusing the supermarket for gourmet delights and toilet paper, Jenny and Trevor were accosted by a tall dark and handsome Frenchman "Are you Engleesh please?" he enquired.

"My name is Fabrice and I will like to practice my Engleesh wiz you please."

In the conversation that followed, which alternated between fractured English, and mutilated French, Jenny and Trevor explained how we were marooned at the local port de plaisance and invited Fabrice to visit us aboard.

Not really expecting a normally reticent Frenchman to follow up on such an offer, we were pleasantly surprised when later that day, there was a knock on the door and there he was. Fabrice late of the supermarket and a recently retired diesel mechanic from the *Légion Etrangère*.

Fabrice was considering working as a mechanic in Western Australia and wanted to discuss job possibilities in the Outback. He was to become our very first real French friend and we welcomed him aboard for a very amusing conversation.

Over coffee, Fabrice mangled English and we butchered French but somehow communicated and there was much laughter as he told us about his life in the foreign legion, in exchange for information about the iron ore mines of our home state.

That night I was woken by a big splash outside,from the watery thrashing outside it sounded as if a late night reveller had fallen in the water after a goon bag of wine too many. I got up to investigate but by the time I arrived on deck the noise had ceased. Either the offender had drowned quietly, which was very considerate of them, or it was a false alarm so I made my way back below. No sooner had I climbed under the covers, than again there was a splashing in the water outside. This time it carried on longer and the absence of a voice, made me suspect that either someone was playing silly buggers, or perhaps a passing dog had fallen in the canal. Back on deck I went, but it was pitch black outside and there was still no sign of the perpetrator and the water around the boat appeared undisturbed.

On and off night the mysterious splashing continued through the night and eventually I gave up looking for the source, pulled my pillow over my head and went back to sleep.

The next morning as I was heading to the shower block, I met Jacques the harbour manager on his way to work and I asked about the mysterious nocturnal disturbances.

"Oh la la," said Jacques with a wry Gallic grin *"C'est l'amour naturellement*, ze ow you say, fucking fish are fucking!"

Apparently, a species of large catfish resident in the Bassin become very amorous in mating season and in a strange ritual they leap out of the water, thus making quite a racket. These were the culprits responsible for our sleepless night, but it certainly explained the large number of overnight fishermen who were camped around the banks of the Grand Bassin in their pop up tents. They were all hoping to hook a hot lover for dinner.

A few days later our legionnaire Fabrice returned with his son and his equally handsome friend Jean-Paul, they arrived bearing Champagne and roses for the ladies. There was a yellow rose for Jenny and a red rose for Trish. Our two matrons instantly turned into giggling schoolgirls, swooning from the devastating effect of two handsome gift bearing Frenchmen.

Later when the Gallic charmers had gone, both ladies made it very clear that the bar had now been lifted and Trevor and I would have to raise our romantic game to compete on French soil. Our recent romantic gifts of a new impeller for the engine and a whistling kettle for the galley, had totally failed to impress our brides.

A few days later on Fabrices' recommendation we attended an open day at the usually secretive nearby Foreign Legion base. Once a year the mysterious military brotherhood opens its barrack gates for a garden fête for friends and family to celebrate the Battle of Camarón.

It was in Mexico 1863 that the foreign legion really earned its legendary status, when a company of some 65 men led by Captain Jean Danjou was besieged by two thousand revolutionaries in the Hacienda Camarón. Bravely, the legionnaires fought against these massive odds until only six men remained alive. Out of ammunition, rather than surrender, these six conducted a bayonet charge against the overwhelming enemy. The surviving two legionnaires were spared by the Mexican general, who allowed them to return to France as an honour guard for their dead commander Captain Danjou.

As a footnote to the battle, Captain Danjou apparently had a wooden hand, which was nicked during the fighting, but which was later returned to the Legions Museum at Aubagne. Today it is paraded annually on Camerone Day as the most precious relic of the legion.

Just as bizarre as the sacred hand of Capitaine Danjou, were the stalls of the fête. Fairy floss and toffee apple displays rubbed shoulders with tables of rocket propelled grenades and machine guns in a carnival that couldn't make up it's mind if it was an arms convention, or a miniature Disneyland.

During the afternoon, heavily armed parachutists free fell into the centre of a parade ground, while oblivious chubby children rode a merry go round and ate massive legionnaire sandwiches, which are baguettes stuffed with spicy Merguez sausage and French fries. These were cooked in camouflaged mobile mess hall tents. It was a rather unusual family outing to say the least. But the locals were in good festive cheer seemingly unaffected by all the tools of death and destruction that were festooned about as party decorations.

Some days later, whilst buying our customary morning bag of fresh croissants, from the *boulangérie*, I noticed a poster adjacent the delectable pastries, that advertised a *Vide Grenier* to be held the following day in the nearby village of Payra sur l'Hers. There were more of the posters in the bricolage and also in our usual cafés, but I didn't understand what they were promoting though the prevalence of advertising suggested it was an event of some importance. Our dictionary translated *Vide Grenier* as "Empty Attic", which I didn't find at all helpful or informative, so I went off to the marina office to consult Michelle the multilingual receptionist.

Michelle is one of those annoyingly talented European polyglots who can take a phone call in Dutch, whilst answering a fax in German, keep her French boss happy with friendly chat and simultaneously explain things to us in fluent English.

Michelle explained that spring is the season of the *Vide Grenier*, a sort of car boot junk sale for the whole village, where everyone brings the things they no longer want or use and they set up stalls in the streets to sell them. Village streets are crammed with the unwanted contents of attics, cupboards and garages. Children run around fossicking in the piles for cheap toys, whilst adults swap their junk for someone else's.

One can find everything for sale at a *Vide Grenier*, from a motorbike, to books and bric a brac of all shapes and sizes. Local sellers are also often augmented by the presence of commercial merchants who purvey antiques of dubious provenance to the unwary, or arrive searching for authentic treasures to resell in big city antique shops.

The whole concept sounded brilliant, so I asked Michelle for directions to the village of Payra sur l'Hers 'Oh it is so simple,' she said. 'It is only fifteen kilometres away."

Early the following morning, Trevor and I set off by bicycle for the village determined to search for a bargain.

Pedalling along comfortably under a clear blue sky we made our way out of town, past the railway station on the outskirts of town, past the old power station with its broken windows and were soon passing through green fields of pasture which alternated with crops of healthy young maize. Up a gentle rise we cycled towards a line of fringing hills in the near distance.

At first the road was shaded by tall Australian eucalyptus trees, which reminded us of home. The gum tree is particularly hardy, capable of withstanding the long dry periods of summer and has the added advantage of not shedding its leaves, so it provides good shade all year round. Not surprisingly these have now become very popular foliage in southern parts of Europe but to us the juxtaposition and noticeable absence of kangaroos seemed a bit weird.

After two kilometres of easy travel, we passed over a bridge and the road became progressively steeper, as we headed uphill on a long steep incline, that brought Stairway to Heaven to mind. The gradient increased consistently as we ground on and upwards. It was mid morning and the sun beat down hotter and hotter, so that soon we were both sweating profusely and puffing like Thomas the Tank engine going up Mont Blanc.

What Michelle had neglected to tell us, was that Payra sur l'Hers was a hilltop village and though it was indeed only fifteen kilometres away, twelve of those kilometres were straight uphill and our gentlemanly cycle excursion had turned into what felt to us like the mountain ascent section of the Tour de France.

After a couple of hours of alternately riding and pushing our bikes up the steepest bits, we finally located the village. It was an absolute gem, rather like the town that time forgot, straight out of the pages of a romantic French novel.

An intricate maze of winding streets all somehow converged to meet at the ancient *église* on the summit of a hill. From outside this small church a panoramic view in all directions extended over the valley, revealing the tiny river Hers below winding through the cornfields like a silver snail trail. Our hard slog to get there was rewarded by the magnificence of the view.

But we had come for the bargains and sure enough as promised every villager had indeed emptied their attic and the narrow streets were bursting with trash and treasures of all kinds. We set to browsing in earnest and it wasn't long before I had bought a pair of mechanics overalls for a mere €5. In these classic French olive coveralls with double zips up the front, all I would need now would be a fag drooping from the corner of my mouth, a beret and a few choice oil stains and I could pass myself off as the village idiot mechanic.

While I tried on my grease monkey fiery, Trevor who is an excellent cook, was overjoyed to have unearthed a pile of French recipe books. Amongst them a copy of the Larousse Gastronomique, the bible of French cooking and a sacred text amongst gastronomes everywhere. He couldn't believe his luck and pounced like a tiger on a wounded gazelle before anyone else spotted it.

We spent several pleasant hours rummaging through the jumble, finding so many useful things, but in the end we were limited by what we could carry home on our bikes, so we called a halt and went off in search of something to eat.

We didn't have to look far. For lunch the local farmers had lit a brazier filled with gnarled vine roots over whose glowing coals they now were cooking the delicious local Merguez sausages we had enjoyed with the legionnaires. We were soon ensconced under a shady tree outside the community hall with large sausage and baguette rolls and a couple of large beers refuelling for the trip back to the boat.

After a leisurely lunch and a couple more cleansing beers, it was time to leave. We strapped our new treasures to the iron stallions and boarded them for the return. What a difference that return journey was, it was downhill all the way.

Unfortunately, as he picked up speed, Trevor discovered that the brakes on his venerable steed didn't work. The colour rapidly drained from his face and he was experiencing a white knuckle and brown trousers moment. Unable to stop, Trevor held on for grim death as his baggy board shorts flapped wildly in the wind like wings. He broke through the sound barrier at Mach 1.5 and hurtled down the hill seconds away from almost certain destruction as he took each hairpin bend at impossible speeds. Incredibly, he held it together and whilst I suspect a little pee may have emerged at one point, when he finally reached the base of the hills unscathed he looked exhilarated and euphoric.

"Bloody hell mate, that was good, we should do it again! "

The rest of the ride was uneventful and were soon back on board in Castelnaudary proudly displaying our spoils to the girls and ready for the evening Pastis session,

We had now been in Castelnaudary for much longer than we had intended and after breakfast one morning as I looked at the neighbouring barges moored nearby with their permanent power connections and quayside mailboxes that had settled here for the duration, I realised we were in danger of becoming fixtures ourselves. Charmed by the *Chaurienne* locals as we were, if we were to succeed in our mission of sailing to Paris we needed to unmoor tout de suite and get going. There was nothing for it, it was time to tackle the bureaucracy, get our French skippers tickets and set sail. But should we begin?

Load up the rubber bullets

10cc

All was not well in our legal department. While we were making our new home weatherproof and continuing to subsidise the local *laverie* and bricolage, I had been trying to find out what paperwork would satisfy the French waterways authorities and permit us to cruise unmolested across the France to Paris. So far my efforts and enquiries had been a failure of epic proportions as one department hand balled me to another and on it went.

Before leaving Australia I sought advice from several canal gurus, but their opinions had all differed. Twenty assorted wise men gave me twenty different answers.

'Register the boat in Australia and use your Oz skippers ticket,' said one sage.

'Rubbish, much better to register the boat in England and get a Royal Yachting Association Certificate,' said another.

'Don't bother, no one will check, it is France after all," commented a third.

Many canal veterans waxed lyrical about their long held French licenses, cryptically called the Permis C or PP's, but even they weren't sure of the current rules.

François an Australian expatriate of French heritage and a long term bargee explained how in his fluent French he had once asked the water police for an explanation. After some weeks of detective work even they couldn't give him a definite answer and with a wink

39

and a shrug of the shoulders they suggested that, "Perhaps you don't worry about it too much."

This attitude is very French until something goes wrong and then if the paperwork is out of order it may be a very different story. The prospect of a French gaol and a large hairy cellmate who wanted to play Mummies and Daddies didn't sound attractive, so I decided to do the right thing by the authorities, if only I could find out just what that meant.

Persistent sleuthing that would have impressed Sherlock Holmes, finally revealed the existence of an EEC agreement to standardise boating licenses across the continent of Europe. Laws, signage and licences were all to take on the homogeneity of the rest of border free Europe.

However, like much of the Utopian legislation vomiting out of the EU parliament in Strasbourg, the implementation of this particular decision had dragged in the bureaucracies of the participating countries and now nobody really knew what was going on. The result was about as effective as Greek fiscal policy.

In typical fashion, Paris had agreed to the Euro policy and then unilaterally decided to implement bits of it and not others in their own unique way, because it was decided that some of the signage just wasn't French enough.

After exhausting all avenues of enquiry in Oz, I eventually decided there was only one thing for us to do; Procrastinate! I would battle the problem once we arrived in France.

A month prior, when Trevor our advance guard arrived in Paris, he decided to go in search of the elusive skippers license before setting off to view the boat in Castelnaudary,

Picture yourself in his place, you are armed with unbridled enthusiasm, but with very limited French and a phrase book that is entitled 'French for Dummies.' You are setting out on a quest to make sense of

Parisian bureaucracy, a subject not even the French can fathom, and you have only two days in which to do it.

Trevor's mission took him on a Cooks tour of the officialdom of France, as he bounced unsuccessfully from one bureau to the next, until finally he was steered to the head office of the canal authority, the *Voies Navigable de France* (VNF). Even there at the temple of the inland waterways, nobody would give him an unequivocal answer and certainly not one that an Anglophone could hope to understand.

After two days of schlepping around Paris and almost a broken man, Trevor managed to purchase a book of exam revision notes for something called the *Permis Plaisance Fluvial*. He was none too certain what this actually was, whether it was what we needed, or even how to get it if it was, but it felt like a result.

Now many weeks later as we were finishing our boat repairs in Castelnaudary, Frèdèric the boat broker generously agreed to help us navigate the French license system and to solve the skippers ticket mystery. He assured us that for him it would be no problem and we poor naïve fools believed him.

Frèdèric's office was located in the large loft of an old barn overlooking the Grand Bassin. A beautiful open planned area, its ancient oak timber beams and historical architecture contrasted with the modern computer work stations of the charter company, whose headquarters occupied its space. Unfortunately, the architects had been so focussed on their need to produce a visually stunning environment, that they forgot vital details like windows and insulation. The result was an inefficient air-conditioning system which rendered the claustrophobic loft like the North Pole in winter and the Sahara in summer.

So there we sat freezing in our spring clothing surrounded by office staff in coats and anoraks, as Frèdèric started making phone calls on our behalf. He

41

began by trying to see if our Australian permits would be recognised by the local authorities and he commenced the bureaucratic run around. After three unsuccessful calls we could see that this was going to take quite some time, our fear of frostbite got the better of us and so we left him to it.

In the end it took Frèdéric two days to get an answer to our problem and when it arrived it wasn't the response we had hoped for. None of our qualifications, not even my Yachtmasters certificate would be recognised by the authorities. To drive a French registered boat in France, the VNF insisted on a French Skippers License. The mere mentioning of this hallowed paper in the presence of canal bureaucrats caused their eyes to glaze over and elicited warm nods of approval.

So if this was the magic paper, fine so be it, but how did we get one?

Frèdéric assured us that it would be easy, all that was required was a simple test, albeit in French and he knew a man who could arrange everything, so a booking was to be made to take the test in two week's time. Matters were in hand at last, or so we thought.

Out came the regulations revision book that Trevor had bought in Paris and we set to work to study it. It was soon obvious that the theory component was pretty easy once we translated it, there were brain smashers like 'What does a no entry sign mean?' However, it was actually understanding the questions that was going to be the tricky part. Small changes in the syntax of a question could mean a 180 degree change in the answer.

'How do you decide which is the right bank of a canal and which is the left?' I asked Trevor.

'Depends if you are looking upstream or downstream mate'

Many boating terms didn't appear in the Larousse dictionary. For example what the heck is a *'Bief de partage'* is it:

A. A casserole of partridge
B. An argument with your partner
C. The highest section of a canal

(Answer: C)

For the next fortnight we bashed the dictionary trying to make sense of the regulations manual and its colloquialisms.
In the meantime, it was very frustrating to be unable to leave the dock as we watched a parade of inexperienced rental skippers cruise erratically by. The boating skill of some of these punters left a lot to be desired, as they regularly crashed their boats into our jetty. Others trying clumsily to berth their boats, had us up on deck in a flash to fend them off and avoid damage to our precious Challenger One.
Most memorably one day a large party of rotund Germans arrived at the marina for a holiday. They had brought boating supplies from home, which consisted exclusively of beer and sausage. After a salutary twenty minute briefing from the rental base staff, beers were opened and an impromptu Oktoberfest was soon in full swing aboard.
"Ein Prosit, Ein prosit die Gemüchlichkeit...." they sang as one toast followed another and the Löwenbräu flowed freely. After an hour or two of alcoholic conditioning they decided they were ready for the off.
Remembering to cast off the shore lines, they slammed the motor into fast forward and the boat shot out of its berth like a turbo charged Panzer on vacation to Poland. Out into the Grand Bassin pond they accelerated and headed for the bridge archway at the southern end of the harbour. At hull speed the Krauts rocketed under the bridge, only to find that the canal takes a tight left hand bend. Alarmed but undeterred by this abrupt surprise, they threw the helm to port and

43

swerved drunkenly around the corner. As they did so the boat heeled over and pitched a big percentage of their Oktoberfest into the green waters of the canal. They were so busy surviving this unexpected turn that they failed to notice the lock gates ahead of them were closed and traveling at blitzkrieg speed they were unable to stop in time or turn in the narrow canal. They had nowhere to go but right smack into the gates and that's what they did.

Incredibly, instead of shattering into a collection of fibreglass shards the boat rode up over the lock gates and became wedged on top of them where it hung suspended like a shag on a rock, whilst the crew, suddenly sober, teetered there wondering what the heck to do next.

It took three days at the height of tourist season to free the stranded boat and reestablish thoroughfare of the Canal du Midi, the busiest tourist waterway in France.

What happened to the German crew you might ask? Unbelievably, once rescued from their perch on top of the gates, the rental company gave them another boat, wished them well and they were last seen disappearing over the horizon in the opposite direction in a cloud of bratwürst, sauerkraut and pretzels.

Though rental skippers often provide us much amusement and deserve their unofficial title of "Bumpers", the regular bargees, are not without their own characteristics or foibles. In the interests of evenhanded reporting I will pause my narrative here to make the following politically incorrect and highly biased generalisations of some national traits we have observed on the waterways.

The Dutch
The lads from the Zuyder Zee have a bad name with the French, who don't like them because they have a well deserved reputation for being stingy. One Frog said the Dutch make the Scots look like big spenders.

Dutchmen are always looking for a free port and when they find one the word goes out to their countrymen and the next thing you know the place is chock a block with Cloggies. They overstay their welcome and buy nothing in the local shops, which doesn't endear them to the village merchants. On the plus side they almost all speak English and are good to share a beer with. (Dutch beer bought in Holland of course.)

Spanish

Spaniards are rarely seen on the canals they prefer the Mediterranean, where they can look cool with great tans, wrap around sunglasses and can ponce around on pencil thin speedboats that look like they should be running drugs into Miami. The Dons local reputation is that they don't listen and travel everywhere at top speed as if their paella was on fire. Their absence from French canals is probably an aesthetic loss because young Spanish women are arguably the most beautiful in the world. Gorgeous when young, they come with a definite use by date and somehow self-destruct and turn into their rotund grandmothers on their thirtieth birthdays.

Italians

I have never seen one. The Dings are a parochial lot, who like the French, believe their food and wine to be the best in the world and the only fare worth consuming, so why would they leave Italy? They stay at home with their Mamas.

Russians

The Ivans are also rare birds on French waterways, they prefer laundering their roubles at the overpriced Dior, Chanel and Prada haute couture shops of Paris. They are disliked for wearing plumage with excessive bling, not speaking any language but Russian and then looking pissed off when no one understands them. Because these Russian Mafia expats are used to getting things their own way at home, they keep to themselves which is probably for the best.

Brits
Usually a cheerful lot and good company, despite the obvious handicap of being Poms.

Very territorial. A recent French newspaper article showed a distribution pattern of expatriate Poms running down the coast to the Med in the south, but virtually none living in the east or the centre of the country. Like migratory birds many take the River Saône/Rhone route to go from the UK to the Med on yachts, or flock together around St Jean De Losne. Here they are a reliable source of Gin and Tonic at any time of day a talent not to be undervalued

In the east near Germany and Luxembourg sightings are rare to non-existent because fundamentally Brits are birds attracted to the warmer drier southern climes.

Irish
Haven't invented the boat yet, or heard of France. They go to Germany and open Irish pubs.

Americans
Yanks are an endangered species that came close to extinction in Europe during the Bush years. Following 9/11 the Americans left Europe in droves, anti Bush sentiment was high in France and it was not considered prudent to fly the Stars and Stripes on a boat. Since Obama's reign, things have changed with a small number of pioneers returning. Thus a timid pennant size US flag, is occasionally sighted on Yank privateers. Our experience with boating Americans in France has been that only the most adventurous souls are venturing back at the moment, they keep their loud accents and Bermuda shorts well concealed and so consequently they are usually good value.

Danes

There are lots of Danes in eastern France. These guys are great. Usually very experienced mariners, we have encountered no less than three retired ships captains. Because nobody speaks Danish they all have great English and love nothing better than to share schnapps and a few beers. Do not try and match these guys drink for drink, unless you fancy undergoing dialysis and a liver transplant.

Swedes

'Why are they all named Sven or Ingrid (See also Danes above.)

Germans

The sausage munchers are mainly seen habituating the canals that connect with the Rhine. Germans are hardy souls and usually good sailors; they have to be, to travel on the swirling torrent of the Rhine. The most popular run for Krauts goes up the Rhine to Strasbourg, into the Canal Rhone au Rhin, west to Nancy, north on the Moselle, then to the Sarre and back to Strasbourg and home. Its proponents affectionately know this as the "Sauerkraut Route".

Easily recognised by wearing high socks with sandals, big beer gut in the male of the species and excessive displays of voluminous flesh in the females, they insist on swimming and showering naked in public. Disturbing!

Australians

Bloody brilliant magnificent creatures. No seriously folks, anyone who crosses the planet to live on a small floating box in an inferior climate must be either some sort of nutter or a dead-set legend. I prefer the latter description. Whilst the biggest concentration of Aussies, is seen in the Burgundy and west half of France, occasional sighting of specimens off the beaten track and in the far north are also not uncommon. Socially gregarious creatures.

Kiwis
Rare, brilliant like Aussies, but not quite as good.

Meanwhile back in Castelnaudary, there were now only two days left before we were due to sit the theory examination for our skippers tickets. Our test was to take place in the small Mediterranean town of Marseillan, over two hundred kilometres away and so a hire car would be required for the three hour drive to get there and a smart yellow little Citroën was booked for the occasion
The big day arrived and first thing in the morning I walked up the quay to the barn loft office and asked Frédéric to phone the authorities to confirm that our test arrangements were in order before we left.
Half an hour later an unusually subdued Frédéric knocked on our door.
"I am very sorry, zer will be no test' he said. 'I did not understand that you wished me to actually make ze booking for you and so it has not been arranged.'
This news was about as welcome as a fart in a space suit. After two weeks of preparatory study and hours spent translating obscure French boating terms into English, Trevor and I were gutted. It seemed as if the intangible captains licenses would continue to elude us.
Looking very sheepish as well he should, Frèdéric apologised profusely and promised to arrange a new rendezvous for the following fortnight.
Poor old Trevor was supposed to be in Spain by then, walking the pilgrims trail to visit the sacred relics of Saint Jimmy the Fish in Santiago De Compostela. To be in Marseillan for the new test date would now mean an additional return air fare back to France. These

licenses were becoming a very expensive as well as an elusive exercise.

Naturally, we intrepid mariners rallied well in the face of adversity, dried our tears, toughened up and two weeks later Frèdéric was once more asked to confirm the new rendezvous before we left to drive to Marseillan.

Ten minutes later a very contrite Frèdéric came aboard our land locked vessel to inform us that the test had been delayed again. This time the exam centre had overbooked and we had been rescheduled to the city of Montpellier in another weeks time. It felt like Groundhog Day, as the same scene was playing out over and over again. On the plus side, Frèdéric had arranged in the meantime for us to sit the practical component of the exam in Marseillan.

Two days later we were ready to embark for the coast but before departing and following our previous disappointments, Trish this time wisely asked Cecile, the Marina receptionist, to confirm with the bateau école that there would be no more delays.

Unbelievably, this time Commandant Marco the instructor in Marseillan, wanted to postpone. The weather in Marseillan was apparently a bit windy and he was afraid of getting his boat wet.

"*N'annullez pas!!!*" insisted Trish in desperation to Cecile. "Tell him, Zer weel be NO cancellation! We are on our way *c'est* unthinkable to call off!"

We climbed into our rented Citroën and set off at top speed for the bateau école on the Mediterranean. The drive to the coast along fast motorways was uneventful and we arrived in plenty of time for our rendezvous with destiny. What a change from the damp of Castelnaudary, Marseillan we discovered to be a charming and scenic small town centred around a harbour with a quayside that was bathed in bright morning sunshine. The idyllic marina was flanked by rows of old stuccoed buildings. Most were painted in sandstone yellow with orange tiled roofs and contained shops, cafes and restaurants that spilled over onto the quay itself. It was still only half past spring, so the summer crowds had not yet descended on the town. Here and there local children were swimming between the moored yachts and fishing boats enjoying a game of chase.

We sat in an al fresco restaurant in front of a building that seemed rather out of place in the setting. At three stories high, it loomed over its single floor neighbours and its tall narrow windows and Mansard roof made it look like it had been transplanted from the streets of far away Paris, sort of Louis XIV meets fishing village. Nevertheless it boasted an excellent restaurant and we set to fortifying ourselves for the examination ordeal ahead with a magnificent lunch. The local seafood was fresh and plentiful, especially the local Étang de Thau oysters the area prides itself on.

We were lingering over our delightful meal when Trish dropped a bombshell and announced she had discovered from the waiter that that this was the wrong Marseillan. The bateau école office that we spotted on arrival in town which was located in an old quayside canal boat, was apparently not a test centre and our test was scheduled in Marseillan Plage and that was six kilometres away, due to start in five minutes, une catastrophe!

Throwing some cash on the table to pay for the unfinished lunch, we jumped into the car and took off like the Stig on steroids. Fifteen minutes later with a trail of speeding tickets and singed asphalt in our wake we arrived at the Marseillan Plage only five minutes late for our *rendez-vous.*

Marseillan Plage was altogether a much less salubrious location than it's parent town. A somewhat sterile nouveau development, it had an air of abandonment that hung over its marina full of expensive, unloved boats that waited forlornly for the annual deluge of high season tourists to arrive in a few months time and then abandon them again just as quickly. Empty pseudo-adobe villas that fronted the harbour were like hollow shells that also waited for the summer fling between July and August when the town comes alive and is transformed by visitors. The French descend on the beaches of the south like locusts all determined to soak up a week of Vitamin D before returning to their drudgery in the north.

At the moment the beach was empty and the wind blew the loose sand, erasing footprints as well as any sign of human habitation. The streets were completely deserted for the midday siesta, as we wandered around looking for the elusive boat school. It didn't take long to find, but when we did, like everything else it was closed. There was no sign of our instructor Commandante Marco either, so we sat in the shade of the école cafe terrace watching spinifex tumbleweeds as they blew off the sand dunes along the beach and down the street, which completed the spaghetti western ghost town scenario perfectly.

Time passed slowly, it was so quiet that I felt I could hear my toenails growing. Eventually, just as we were giving up hope, a short, swarthy man with a Zapata mustachio strolled casually towards us arriving at our table in a cloud of cigarette smoke. He lacked only a parrot and a few dreadlocks to have given Johnny Depp a good run for the money for the part of Captain Jack Sparrow.

"Bonjour mes amis, I am Commandante Marco," he said as, he shook hands and introduced himself as proprietor of both the café and boat school.

"It is not possible to start before we have ze coffee" he insisted in a patois of Franglais.

As Marco's ramshackle coffee shop didn't own a coffee machine, he served us his instant plastic caffeine. I am sure there should be a law against this terrible stuff, it tasted of recycled shopping bags mixed with stewed seaweed. Jenny and Trish wisely declined the

51

Commandante's offer and decided to go elsewhere in search of a less toxic beverage and left us to our fate.

'Messieurs, I am the highest authority for the Permis Fluvial test, I am the supreme authority in nautical matters and you need to speak to no one but me. I will take care of everything.' announced Marco with a flourish.

'Bloody brilliant.' replied a very relieved Trevor.

It seemed the *Permis Fluvial* licenses were in the bag at last. Naturally nothing in France is ever that simple, as much to our chagrin we were about to discover,

"*Desolée*, it is too windy today to take my boat out, the insurance would not cover an accident," apologised Marco. We were gobsmacked, was this yet another delay?

Then without bothering to question our experience, or look at our qualifications the omnipotent one said, 'You boys look like sailors to me, so you pass!'

After this unexpected but very welcome turn of events, all that now remained was for Marco to officially annotate our log books and so we sat in his café and waited for him to rubber stamp us.

Out of respect for our intestines we politely refused another serve of bilge water coffee and waited for him to proceed. Marco puffed acrid Gitanes and stared out to sea. After ten minutes all polite conversation was exhausted, so we just sat and waited in silence. Nothing happened. What was he waiting for? Perhaps the great one was going through the motions of waiting out the one and a half hours theory period that the law specified, so he could accredit us in a modicum of good faith.

We said nothing, Marco said nothing, we all just sat and waited. An hour later we were still waiting. The silence was deafening.

Trish often says I have the patience of a fly in a bottle which is probably true, I hate sitting still, so this forced inactivity was torture for me and it was driving me nuts.

52

I just do not do patience well. It was a Mexican stand off, neither party was prepared to make a move. We certainly weren't shifting without our log books and Marco didn't seem to be in a mood to hand them over. Eventually, I couldn't stand the waiting any longer and asked him if he might be able to stamp our log books now.

"Oh I can't do that, it is not permitted until you have passed ze theory exam first, then you must come back again to Marseillan and I feex everything then. The examining bureaucracy says it is not possible to to pass the practical test before passing the theory test, but we fool them today, non?" explained the Commandante

Not daring to risk displeasure of the self anointed supreme nautical power before the official stamps were actually inked in our log books, Trevor and I submissively bowed our way out of Marco's presence and drove morosely back to Castelnaudary, to await the theory exam the following week.

Though today we had passed the practical exam and logged five hours of sea time by drinking bad coffee and without ever leaving the cafe, it was really just another non result after all. We had not made any tangible progress towards getting our permits and we were still trapped in the rental port unable to legally leave the dock.

The next week seemed to drag by as each day we sat on deck and watched the clients of the rental company depart or return to the base and our sense of frustration at not being able to join them grew logarithmically as each boat passed us by.

Trevor had succumbed to a cold, possibly caught from Jenny, who had it when they returned from Spain and he retreated to his bed armed with pills and whisky. An outbreak of swine flu was rife in Spain at the time, so we treated him like a leper and he was quarantined in the forward cabin with his revision book, and an

53

industrial size box of tissues. Food was periodically thrust at him from a distance as no one was very keen to catch his plague which looked very unpleasant and involved drainage from multiple orifices.

That week, for once it felt good to be securely moored to a jetty as the Tramontane a strong, dry cold wind from the Northwest blew fiercely and it was not pleasant to be out and about.

At last Saturday arrived, Trevor had returned to the living and it was time for the theory test, so off we all went in another rental car on the long drive to Montpellier.

Montpellier really is a special place. What's more, very few people outside France have learned just what a fantastic city it is. Broad boulevards lined with shady plane trees, a huge car-free central square laid out in the 1700s and surrounded by elegant balustraded buildings, there is even a vast triumphal arch. You name it, Montpellier's got it and it's just minutes away from the beach, too. As Languedoc-Roussillon's capital city it is arguably the chicest spot on France's southwest coast, and it certainly pulls in the punters. A large student population means that the nightlife, fashions and café culture cater to the young and shapely, with a reasonable helping of up-market wine bars, modern restaurants and smart stores also targeting the sizeable community of lawyers and doctors. Unfortunately, we were destined to see none of this as we headed to a nondescript concrete office building in the industrial outskirts area of the city for our test.

In France boat and car licence exams are conducted in centralised examining centres spread around the country and in this beautiful city we were booked into one by Commandante Marco. As we had come to do battle with the examiners, it meant that unfortunately enjoying beautiful Montpellier was out of the question. We were men on a mission.

This didn't stop Jenny and Trish who shot off like a couple of Exocet missiles in the direction of the boutiques and cafes.

'Good luck, you'll be right boys, we're offski.'

Again put yourself in our place for a moment. Trevor's French has been self taught from conversational CD's and the Internet. I have only the remnants of high school French that Monsieur Andreotti my mad Italian school master managed to lodge in my little grey cells back in 1968. The theory exam will be entirely in French. The pass mark is 21 out of 25 questions. A miss in a multiple answer question is a total question wrong and failure means we will not be able to take the boat on the canals. No pressure? The success of our whole French adventure depends on the outcome of this exam. To say we were both shakier than a bowl full of jelly would be an understatement. This was crunch time.

Trevor had put in countless hours of study, laboriously memorising every possible permutation of questions as he lay sweating on his death bed full of swine flu. I was now feeling very worried about my total lack of effort. True, I had been seen to open the revision book occasionally and once even held it the right way up, but I am now regretting my lack of preparation.

We rejoin the action, Trevor and I are sitting silently in a waiting room looking like condemned men. There are about twenty other candidates all of whom are French and they all look just as apprehensive. The place looks like the waiting room in a maternity ward full of expectant fathers.

The first exam was scheduled for 9 a.m. and at 10 o'clock ours is to be the second group to face the examiners.

At 9 a.m. the first candidates disappeared into the mysterious exam room at the end of the corridor and heavy soundproof doors closed ominously behind them. In the waiting room the nervous tension in the air amongst the would be skippers was palpable as the remaining candidates sat reading well thumbed rule books and chanting the answers like mantras.

"La rive gauche est à gauche, ou à babord, si on va en aval."

"La rive gauche est à droite, ou à tribord si on va en amont."

So much to remember, if only I'd brought a bigger brain..

The theory tests are a audiovisual format with a time limit of 15 minutes but by 9.55 there was no sign of the first group exiting which was strange. At 10.05 the exam room door opened and out they came. They did not look happy, there was much grumbling and something was obviously wrong.

'L'ordinateur ne marche pas,'

Eventually, we gleaned that after the first question the computer generating the questions had spat the dummy and died. The 9 a.m. group was told to wait pending arrival of *le mécanicien* So we waited too.

10.30 a.m. came and went, 11 a.m. came and went. Finally at 11.30 madame the examiner emerged from her lair and hiding behind a large florid faced security guard, she proceeded to inform the disgruntled nine o'clock group that their test had been cancelled and they would all have to come back in two weeks time.

Our group was told to wait until further notice. After all we had gone through over the last month with the numerous delays, not to mention the two hour drive just to get to Montpellier today, it looked as if there would be yet another disappointing postponement.

At this stage Trevor and I had had enough and our conversation turned to wild schemes like re-registering the boat in Panama, or even Australia and using Australian recreational skippers tickets, bugger the French. We were both aware that this might be problematic when crossing borders and would likely lead to bigger problems in the future. Nevertheless, we had just about had it with trying to comply with French regulations.

Noon approached and the cut off time of the midi siesta would soon be upon us and that would mean game over for today. Everything in the south of France closes tighter than a Scotsman's purse for midday, so if the computer was not fixed in the next few minutes there would be no option but to reschedule.

At one minute to noon, just when all hope seemed to be gone, madame emerged and contrary to our expectations announced , ''The computer system may now work, will candidates please enter the exam room tout de suite and we will give it ze try .'

With the our fellow applicants who were just as pissed off about the delay as we were, we bolted through the soundproofed doors of doom and entered the exam room nearly trampling the examiner underfoot in a rush, before she could change her mind.

Once in the chamber, each candidate submitted their logbook and an ID to madame who in her severe black dress and with her hair tied up in a bun, sat behind a school teachers desk like Madame Defarge doing her knitting while taking in guillotine executions in Charles Dickens's "Tale of Two Cities". She handed each candidate an electronic answer box with a small LCD screen and six unmarked coloured buttons.

The exam room itself was a tiered lecture theatre with parallel rows of plastic theatre seats that faced a large projection screen, and we were told to space ourselves out so that there could be no collusion over answers.

When everyone was seated and without a word of apology for the delay, Madame launched into a machine gun speed French description of the exam procedure which ended with the statement,

"Comprenez-vous?" Does everyone understand?

"Non!" I replied and all heads turned towards me.

"S'il vous plait répétez plus lentement madame,"

It was obvious to the other French candidates, none of whom were now well disposed towards Madame, that there were foreigners in their midst and I could sense an air of sympathy from these comrades in arms, in our moment of adversity.   In response to my request Madame repeated her litany slowly at first, but after the first sentence she was back up to the same TGV speed as before.

"Comprenez-vous?" Does everyone understand?

"Non!!" I said. The examiner seemed to sense that rest of the class after being messed around for so long was on my side and perhaps a revolution may be in the offing.

"Si vous ne comprenez pas Français ,c'est votre problème M'sieu." She replied. In effect..., too bad!! There was a discontented rumbling from the assemblage, unhappy that one of their number was being treated badly by their tormentor.

We were to discover later that this interjection may have caused more of a stir than we realised at the time. As we left the exam room we noticed that there were three police vans full of the heavy mob of armed Gendarmes parked outside. Jenny later explained that the riot squad had arrived not long after we entered the inquisition, helicopters were whirring overhead and she was worried about what was going on inside. Coincidence, or had they been called up to sort out the foreigners?

The exam was finally underway and questions flashed up on a screen at the front of the auditorium and we pressed the appropriate buttons on our machines to record our answers. Some were trick questions with multiple responses and each question had a short time limit in which to answer before the next one appeared.

Sweat was running down my back and when one particularly difficult French phrasing was used, I peeked sideways to see how Trevor was coping with it and saw his jaw set in grim determination.

After what seemed the longest twenty minutes of my life, finally it was over and we were summoned one by one to Madames' desk. Here she took each answer machine and after checking the score she either placed the vital pass stamp in the license book of the blessed, or dismissed the unlucky candidate with an invitation to return again and have another go.

There were four candidates before me. Two passed, two failed. So it was fifty fifty odds and then it was my turn, so I trudged up to the teachers desk with leaden legs like a man on his way to the scaffold, I handed over my box and waited.

Madame Defarge deliberated over the answers of the foreign interloper, time moved at escargot pace and then reluctantly she picked up her stamp and stamped my book. Hallelujah! I had passed.

Trevor was next in line. His box was scrutinised even more rigorously as the examiners eyes widened visibly, then a stunned grimace slowly spread over her face and with a begrudging acceptance she stamped his book too. It was another pass!

We compared notes later and realised we had both achieved perfect scores and this is what had so amazed Madame, that two Aussies without a Frogs leg to stand on had achieved perfect results when locals were failing to pass.

Now there was only one thing left to do to obtain our *Permis*, and that was to present our log books to Commandante Marco in Marseillan and get the remaining stamp he had promised us for the imaginary practical test.

Arriving in Marseillon Plage later that same afternoon, there were big changes at the combined café and bateau school. The café now had a bar with a bamboo awning and it actually looked quite nice. True to disorganised form, Marco still only had plastic coffee and there was no ice cream to sell in his refrigerator but the Commandante greeted us warmly as old friends, we embraced and kisses were exchanged. (No tongues fortunately.)

Marco again fuelled himself up with the mandatory caffeinated dishwater, which we both politely declined and at last he placed the invaluable stamps and validated into licence books. Trevor and I were now Chevaliers of the *Permis Plaisance Fluvial de France.* Huzzah!!

After all the stress and emotion leading up to the test, the drive back to Castelnaudary was a strangely sober and anticlimactic experience. I clutched the steering wheel and looked catatonically ahead at the road in stunned silence. Trevor was in shock, he just sat rigid in the back seat muttering a mantra over and over "I can't believe we passed, I just can't believe it. "

And that's how it happened. It took Trevor and I five weeks to get our *Permis Fluvial.* It was a major undertaking, but now at last we were licensed to go anywhere on the inland waterways of Europe all 16,000 kilometres of them.

" Look out Paris, we're on our way."

Everything is easy with 20/20 hindsight, and so dear reader for those of you who might be contemplating cruising your own boat in France, here is what you can do to avoid our license drama.

Before leaving home get the revision guide book produced by the examination company and learn the questions in French until you can reliably pass them. Then subscribe to the VNF authorised web site which contains an even bigger selection of the 600 possible questions, as well as an online virtual test box like the one used in the exam centres, so you can practice against the time limit.

Before you get to France, contact a bateau école and arrange for them to book a practical test and a theory test. (Allow a couple of months in advance in the busy season.) Explain that you will do the preparation for the theory exam yourself and will not require lessons.

Unlike our instructor Commandante Marco, who rubber-stamped our practical test (though in fairness he was entitled to do so if he was satisfied that his candidates held other valid qualifications or experience,) you probably will have to do the on water component. This is not examinable, or arduous and for anyone with basic boating experience it's a no-brainer.

We had presented our Australian Recreational Skippers tickets and an International Yachtmaster certificate to the VNF offices in Paris and Toulouse and they were not impressed. You will have to do their test to drive a French registered boat freely in France and fair enough too.

The only other way to get a recognised permit is to obtain an International Certificate of Competence (ICC) from the UK Royal Yachting Association with an inland waters CEVNI endorsement. The CEVNI is now available in countries other than the UK and online.

If sailing a non EU registered vessel through the canals in transit from one sea to another, your national credentials will be recognised. This is fine for yachts, but a canal boat looks like a canal boat so you're not fooling anyone if that's what you are driving.   For anyone other than a genuine passage maker if you stray far from the main arterial waterways having a CEVNI is a good idea.

Of course you could just rent a 'bumper' boat which are loads of fun and then you don't have to worry about any of it, low power rental boats are able to cruise *sans Permis* in areas licensed to rental operators across France. But then you would miss some of the fun.

Anchors aweigh

With the our permits now safely in the bag, I couldn't stand being tied to the jetty at Castelnaudary any longer. Like Mr. Toad of Wind in the Willows, I yearned for the thrill of the open road, or in our case the open canal. To celebrate our triumph over the French Water Nazi's, it was agreed that if the rain ever let up, we would take Challenger One out for a trial cruise.

Right on cue next day, as if sensing our mood, the rain stopped and a feeble sun peeked its face cautiously through a break in the hitherto perpetually grey skies. The day of our first voyage had arrived and though it would hardly be conquering the Atlantic in a rubber duck with a broken paddle, it would be a start. We were bound for a run on the adjoining Grand Bassin of Castelnaudary.

At first turn of the key, the motor started with the choked dry rattle that cold diesel motors always make, almost as if they are protesting the disturbance of their slumbers. As it warmed up, the engine soon settled into a comforting rumble as the oil began to circulate and Brutus our mighty fifty-seven *chevaux* power plant came to life. Fifty seven horsepower may not seem like much to power a 14 metre boat, rather like powering a family car with a lawn mower engine, but for the most part canals are still waters with very low speed limits, so a small engine is all that is required.

Five minutes later with Brutus rumbling contentedly, it was time for the off. Trevor and Jenny cast away the stern lines, remembering just in the nick of time to disconnect our umbilical power cord and we pulled away from the quay towards the centre of the Bassin. This was it, we were adrift in our own boat in France, this was what we had been dreaming about for so long, I was so excited I could feel tears of joy welling up in my eyes. Brass marching bands and big emotional moments have that effect on me, I don't know why, they just do.

After all the time we had spent at the moorings, it seemed strange that this boat could also venture out on to the open water and was not just an expensive extension of the jetty into which we continually poured money and congealed sweat.

I tried a few turning manoeuvres and soon realised that the boat steered like a piece of dangling wet spaghetti. She did not want to travel in a straight line, no matter what I tried, so we zigzagged an erratic course across the Bassin like a drunken man on pension day. If this kept up we would get breathalysed by every passing Gendarme with nothing better to do.

The flat bottom of the hull meant there was little lateral resistance to the single propeller grabbing the water as it rotated, this torque was pulling the back of the boat to starboard, with the result we moved forwards in a crabbing motion. Normally one can counteract this with a small rudder adjustment, but Challenger One was a lateral thinker and needed constant tweaking just to go in a straight line. After a few minutes I began to feel the rhythm required to keep the boat pointing straight ahead and soon things were back under control. Confidence restored, I decided to leave the lagoon and headed north towards the main village where there is a Port de Plaisance created for visitors. From our enforced residence in town we knew that the short cobblestone quayside there hosts some very reasonably priced restaurants as well as a branch office of the VNF, all housed in the old stone buildings that line the left bank.

63

To reach the port would require passing under one of the lowest bridges on the Canal Du Midi, a tiny ancient structure whose arch appeared scarcely wider than the boat itself. There didn't appear to be much headroom or margin for error, so hopefully it would be big enough for us to pass under. Many are the sun umbrellas and miscellaneous pieces of deck furniture that have been swept off the deck of unwary boats in transit under such unforgiving obstacles.

As we approached the entrance of the bridge, it became obvious that passage would be like threading a needle, so with the boat still steering like an inebriated snake, I lined the bow up with the opening, accelerated and hoped for the best. Just as we entered, a swan appeared from nowhere and swam directly at us on a kamikaze course, it was honking loudly and then unbelievably, it started trying to peck a hole in the side of the hull. We were under attack! The berserk bird squawked and honked angry battle cries like a deranged banshee. Not used to being assaulted by savage local wildlife, I swerved slightly twisting the boat and the stern crunched against the stonework as we passed under the centre of the bridge, leaving a telltale smear of white fibreglass on the stonework. Our first battle scar perhaps, but the real damage was to my pride and I could swear I saw a satisfied smile on the bill of that bloody swan as it swam away.

We moored to the quay in front of the Port de Plaisance without further problem. The weather was beautiful, with a clear cloudless blue sky and warm enough to sun-bake. Stepping ashore we walked up a hill to see the old windmill, with its panoramic view of the surrounding area and then strolled back down to the Centre-Ville, before returning to the wharf and lunch at Les Dodines, a charming little restaurant on the quay.

The meal prepared by chef Gislaine Louette was fantastic. *Magrét* of duck for three of us and Jenny ordered fresh sardines stuffed with spinach. Main courses were followed by individual *Crème Brulées* in their little terra cotta bowls, whose caramelised sugar coatings had just the right brittleness, as they shattered under our spoons to reveal the double cream goodness of the custard below.

With a superb lunch completed and righteously fortified with good wine, we thanked Madame Louette and waddled back to the boat ready to retrace our course to the Grand Bassin and cast off.

As we emerged from under the town bridge, the killer swan was waiting for us. It launched itself straight at the boat like a homing torpedo and in spite of our attempts to avoid it, it gave the boat a right good pecking and saw us off its patch. Locals later explained that this swan was notorious in town for its ferocious attacks on canal boats. It had once survived an unfortunate encounter with a motor boat that had left it one webbed foot short of a pair. This had turned it into a feathered Long John Silver, a one legged vigilante with a murderous streak toward power boats.

Back at the base, we faced the challenge of mooring in a very confined gap. All the other boats were tied by their sterns to the wharf and packed in like sardines to save space. In our absence our spot seemed to have contracted significantly. This meant that we would have to reverse the into a narrow gap slightly smaller than the size of our boat when berthing. This process is like parking on a Paris street where the arriving car nudges the bumpers of the cars fore and aft until there is enough space to park between them. This is why it is rare to see a car without bumper damage in Paris.

After weeks of watching inept rental captains make a hash of manoeuvring as they tried to thread themselves into tight positions between other boats, now it was our turn. It didn't look too hard, except that at fourteen metres long with only a single propellor and a boat that was helming like wet spaghetti, it would be even more difficult to steer in reverse. To add to the challenge a

65

strong wind had started to blow across the Grand Bassin and anyone who was too timorous about approaching the wharf, would be caught and swept sideways into the moored vessels. I had a case of performance anxiety, chewed my remaining fingernail and hit reverse gear. I needn't have worried, after some very deft and energetic fending off by the crew, Challenger One did us proud and swept into the desired spot with a minimum of fuss and no further loss of face or fibreglass.

Our short maiden voyage around the neighbourhood was a big success, but this was not what we had come to achieve, Paris beckoned us and it was time to leave Castelnaudary. After five weeks of trials, repairs and frustration, at last we could get underway and just in time too as our welcome in the port was wearing a bit thin and our friends at the rental base were beginning to wonder if we would leave or set up a letter box and emigrate.

That night we hosted a farewell drinks party onboard with the mechanics and office staff who had been so kind to us and next morning we cast off our lines. Champs Elysée, we were on our way at last

Next morning the sun was shining and with a surge from a contented sounding Brutus we pulled out into the Grand Bassin, turned to starboard and headed for the bridge that marks the southern exit to the port. Within minutes we arrived at the first lock, to find the gates that had shipwrecked the German Oktoberfest crew were now wide open and ready for us to enter. We were leaving Castelnaudary and heading down the Canal du Midi for a date with the Mediterranean Sea.

The Canal du Midi is 240 km long, connecting the Garonne River to the Étang de Thau on the coast and along with the Canal de Garonne it forms the Canal des Deux Mers that join the Atlantic to the Mediterranean. The fantastic idea of an inland waterway was first considered by the Roman governors of Gaul, and later nursed by successive French monarchs. It was built to serve as a shortcut between the Atlantic and the Mediterranean, thus avoiding the long sea voyage around hostile Spain, Barbary pirates, and a trip that in the seventeenth century took a full month to complete. Its strategic value was obvious and it had been discussed for centuries. King Francis I brought Leonardo da Vinci to France in 1516 and commissioned a survey of a route from the Garonne at Toulouse to the Aude at Carcassone. The major challenge that prevented construction at that time was that no one including the great Leonardo, could figure out how to supply the summit sections with enough water in summer.

In 1662, Pierre-Paul Riquet, a tax collector in the Languedoc region, who knew the area intimately, believed he could solve the problem. To help in his design, Riquet is said to have constructed a miniature canal in the grounds of his house, complete with locks, weirs, feeder channels and even a tunnel. Google Streetview has a scrambler of peoples' faces to protect their privacy, currently it masks the visage of the creator of the Canal du Midi on a banner displayed outside the canal museum at Saint-Ferréol. This prompted me to send the following email.   "Dear Monsieur Google, Please unmask Pierre Paul Riquet, as he died in 1680, you're probably safe from any legal action!"

Once constructed the system was a masterpiece of both hydraulic and structural engineering. At its peak 12,000 labourers worked on the project, including over a thousand women, many of whom came specifically to work on the water supply system. The women labourers were surprisingly important to the canal's engineering. Many came from former Roman bath colonies in the Pyrenees, where elements of classical construction had been maintained as a living tradition. Building a navigational canal across the continent was well beyond the formal knowledge of the military engineers expected to supervise it, but the peasant women who understood the classical Roman hydraulic methods, added to the repertoire of available techniques. They not only perfected the water supply system for the canal but also threaded the waterway through the mountains near Béziers, using few locks, and built a seven-lock staircase which is still in use today at Fonsérannes just outside of Beziers itself. This was all a bit of a knee trimmer for male French egos, but it was girls who got the job done.

The Canal du Midi was opened officially in 1681. Unfortunately, Riquet never saw it completed, he joined the celestial choir in 1680, just months before the Canal was opened. Today the Midi canal runs from the city of Toulouse down to the Mediterranean port of Sète which was founded to serve as the eastern terminus of the waterway.

The locks on the canal du Midi are a distinctive oval shape constricted at the entrance and exit and flared in the middle. This design was intended to resist the collapse of the walls that happened early in the project. The oval locks use the strength of the arch against the inward pressure of the surrounding soil that had destabilised the early locks built with straight walls. Such arches had been used by the Romans for retaining walls in Gaul, so though this technique was not new, its application to locks was revolutionary and was imitated in early American canals before the arrival of reinforced concrete.

Unfortunately, the oval shape proved quite literally a pain in the backside for Challenger One. At 14 metres in length the shape of these locks meant that when entering if I tried to steer for one side to get a rope ashore, the stern of the boat would swerve the other way and crash into the entry gate on the other side as it passed through. Our first attempted lock entry resembled a dodgem car bumping its way about. The lock keeper raised his eyes skywards in frustration.

"Mon Dieu, les touristes folles."

Despite our ragged entry, we soon had ropes secured fore and aft, the *éclusier* closed the gate behind us and started to empty the lock. We would be traveling downstream towards the Mediterranean, so all locks would be emptying as we descended from the high country towards the sea. This is always easier, because on arrival in the lock, one can step ashore to secure a rope to the bollards on the quay. On ascending locks we would later discover that sometimes one had to scale wet slimy ladders up the lock wall just to get a rope ashore.

Down we went as water flooded out of the chamber and the lengthening side walls loomed above us, till it felt like we were in the bottom of an empty swimming pool. Once the lock was empty, the large steel gates at the far end began to open in front of us. It was reminiscent of the scene in the movie Jurassic Park, when the huge park gates slowly part to admit the unsuspecting travellers to a brave new world. Right on cue as our doors opened Trish announced.

"Mesdames et Messieurs bienvenue á Jurassic Parc."

There stretching straight out in front of us was the first real section of our canal journey to Paris. On the left bank was a canal path, once the towpath for the horse teams that pulled the working *péniches*, now transformed into a cycle way and walking path for the locals. Above us a canopy of leafy green plane trees which were deliberately planted both sides of the canal providing shade and reducing evaporation. The effect of the dappled shade of the trees over the mossy green waters of the canal, was like looking down a verdant tunnel. Beyond the trees on either side stretched fields bursting with sunflowers and rich summer crops. This was the stuff of picture books, the only way to travel and see the real France, not for us busy roads, car fumes and motorways.

69

I sat at the helm enjoying the moment, unfettered by the schedules, dates and responsibilities of the working world. This was everything I had dreamed of, life doesn't get much better. If happiness is getting what you want and wanting what you get, then I was the king of happy at a fun-fest. There was nowhere else I wanted to be and the day just continued to get better as the canopied canal transported us between one lock and the next.

By late afternoon we arrived in Carcassonne with its amazing castle, much of which was rebuilt in the eighteenth century and has been listed by UNESCO. Utterly spectacular, world-renowned and unmissable, Carcassonne comprises a very large, and intact fortified town known as the Cité, as well as a 13th century 'new' town. In 1849 the Cité was in such a state of disrepair that the government proposed to demolish it, which caused a national outcry. Today its restored walls towers and ramparts whilst lovely from afar, shelter inside the world's best-fortified collection of souvenir shops.

From Carcassonne we had been warned that the canal du Midi can become a busy highway in high season, because it is the most popular canal in France when the rental boats are operating at capacity. As it was still only May, we anticipated no problem and indeed our passage through locks rarely saw us waiting for long.

On the third day of living on the Midi, I woke early to bird song and a buttery aroma that told me the local *boulangérie* was open. We had moored for the night to the bank of the canal in the middle of nowhere. There was also a musky caramel smell coming from the vineyards just beyond the banks. Following local tradition, farmers had spread their *marc*, of pressed grapes skins, among the vines as fertiliser and this added even more to the olfactory pleasures of the new morning.

Over the next few days we floated slowly south, through so many wonderful towns and picturesque villages.

In Homps, we ate a memorable meal at *Le Chat Qui Peche*. By the canal and not far from a small town, the eatery is a lovely old house transformed into a great bistro. The welcome from both the delightful owners and their staff was warm enough to toast cheese on. The clientele was straight out of one of those boulevard farces about provincial life that Parisians inexplicably enjoy. There was the notary having lunch with his mistress, a middle-aged bourgeois couple, Madame with her meringue hair, Monsieur with matching socks and tie and a smattering of excited tourists wearing white socks with sandals, marvelling wide eyed at their good fortune to be part of such a rustic scene.

The principal offering was fresh fish, so after a shared plate of charcuterie, we all had beautifully cooked poisson dishes from the daily catch menu. These were followed by a homemade cheesecake and accompanied by a superb local wine which was recommended by the owner from the cellars of Monsieur Gimie of nearby Capestang.

As French school children learn from annotated classroom maps there's probably no waterway in the world that passes through more gastronomically blessed territory. Almost every town along our route was famous for at least one pedigreed food. The tomatoes of Marmande, the prunes of Agen, the Chasselas grapes of Moissac, the Cassoulet of Castelnaudary, to say nothing of the numerous restaurants and wines.

I never ceased to be amazed by the good food you can find in the middle of nowhere. Next morning, was market day in nearby Olonzac. Like most markets in small towns, the one in Olonzac was huge, spilling out of the village square and down side streets. I am always surprised more by the variety than the quantity.

Do this many different sausages, cheeses, spices, nuts and vegetables actually exist in the real world? The easy conviviality and leisurely pace of each day, along with Trish and Trevor's excellent cooking, were a testament to the pleasures of both slow food and slow travel.

Further south Le Somail has a little stone humpback bridge crossing the canal, the Pont Neuf du Somail. Built in 1773, the term "new bridge" is a bit laughable to an Aussie whose country didn't even exist back then. Nearby classic terra cotta roofed houses with vine covered walls basked in the early summer sunshine and on the quay next to the classic Pont Neuf we found Joy.

Joy was an aptly named septuagenarian widow from England, sitting regally on the dock of a port side cafe. Here she spent all season reclined in a deck chair with a good book and glasses of coffee in the morning and then wine in the afternoon. Joy befriended nautical gypsies like us as they cruised by and then retired at night to her modest boat moored nearby, ready to repeat the whole scene every day throughout the length of summer. What a great life? She was just one of the many characters we would meet on our voyage.

From Le Somail we cruised south-east. Over the next few days, heads ducked low we passed under the oddly shaped canal bridge at Capestang, reputed to be if not the lowest in France, the curvature of its arch certainly makes it the smallest. The bridge is a major challenge for many larger boats some of which have to stop and ask passersby to come aboard to ballast their boats low enough so that they can get underneath its legendary arch.

On we travelled until we eventually came to the staircase of locks at Fonsérannes. Here there are seven locks in a row, one cascading into the next. Down we went and then just at the edge of Béziers, the

Canal du Midi crosses over the top of the River Orb like a motorway flyover.

Béziers has a very dark history. It became a stronghold of the Cathar sect, which upset both the king and the Pope. The Cathars were forcibly suppressed by a Catholic crusade in 1209 lead by a very unpleasant bloke, Simon de Montfort, who resorted to primitive psychological warfare. He ordered his troops to gouge out the eyes of 100 prisoners, cut off their noses and lips, then sendtthem back to the town led by a prisoner with one remaining eye as a warning. Later his forces broke into the town and the population of 20,000 was massacred in its entirety by his forces.

Next stop was the Bassin Rond d'Agde, east of Beziers, the only round lock in the world. We arrived just past noon on a warm June afternoon. The nearby town was drowsy as the last shopkeepers had closed for the important business of lunch. As we waited for our turn to enter the rotunda and descend, I saw that a barge headed in our direction was already rising up in the deep stone-lined lock as if to greet us. Four people were seated at a table on the roof deck of the barge, surrounded by pots of geraniums, and as the rushing waters lifted them into view, I saw that they were sharing a roast chicken, a good-looking cheese tray and a tomato salad. *"Bon appétit!"* shouted the lock keeper, and they waved before gliding out past us.

Now it was our turn. As we cruised into it, the round lock seemed harmless enough, but it was more difficult than it looked. We had been warned that if the wind is blowing, it is easy to get trapped in one quadrant or another, unable to get off and make the turn out through the exit gate. Some places are also subject to big turbulence as the lock fills. Fortunately, as the lock emptied without incident, but when I tried to start Brutus to depart he wouldn't fire up. Could we be out of fuel? Unlike the cruise liner, Queen Elizabeth 2, that moves only six inches for each gallon of diesel that it burns,

Challenger One normally runs on the smell of an oily rag and sips a miserly couple of litres per hour so that didn't seem likely. The lock keeper emerged from his shelter and started giving us the hairy eyeball for messing up his schedule.

"Allez Allez!"

Trevor reached desperately for a paddle and then I noticed that the master power switch had been accidentally tripped. Once turned back on Brutus fired up enthusiastically and we were underway disaster averted.

Next day we arrived at Pointe des Onglous the point where the Canal du Midi exits into the Bassin de Thau, a large open estuary, between Agde and Sète we decided to moor up at the Glenans sailing club at Les Onglous. Very quiet and relaxed, there's even a little informal Étang-side beach so we unshipped our bikes and headed off to explore the town and its surrounds.

In early June everything was still shut for winter and the place was a ghost town with the seaside cafes and tourist shops all boarded up along deserted streets. Not what we had been hoping to find at the ritzy Mediterranean, supposed home of sun bronzed intergalactic playboys and girls. This place wouldn't have got the thumbs up from a bus load of funeral directors. Nevertheless, we had arrived at the southern most part of our journey to Paris.

If it's tourist season, why can't we shoot them?

George Carlin

In June Trevor and Jenny abandoned ship to go hiking in the mountains of Spain. They had decided to make a pilgrimage to visit the holy remains of St James the apostle. The Way of Saint James is a web of converging routes that cross Western Europe and arrive at Northern Spain. Pilgrims follow a trail of scallop shell markers across the continent and eventually all trails arrive at the city of Santiago de Compostela. Punters who choose to walk there and pay their respects to the bones of St James, will apparently receive heavenly points in the afterlife and even get a stamped passport to prove it.

As a confirmed heathen I found the whole business a trifle suspect. Firstly, as a saint, James wasn't a raging success. Credited in the conversion game with a measly score of two, he was told off for over enthusiasm by Jesus when he wanted to call down heavenly fire on a Samaritan town and incinerate the locals who had annoyed him a bit. James the fisherman, hereafter referred to as "Jimmy the Fish", was hardly a prize pin up boy for Christianity. He eventually came to a sticky end when King Herod had his head removed, presumably for terrorist leanings and a penchant for pyromania.

Spanish legend has it that for reasons unknown his remains were brought to Spain for burial. According to

75

another medieval tale, some eight hundred years later, the light of a bright star guided a shepherd who was watching his flock at night to this long lost burial site in Santiago de Compostela. The shepherd quickly reported his discovery to the local Bishop Teodomiro. This bloke was no chump, when faced with an unidentified headless corpse and probably a mound of associated paperwork accompanying it, he brilliantly saw this as irrefutable evidence that the remains were those of the late apostle James. Being a bit of an entrepreneur the bishop also realised the economic benefits of having a stash of holy relics on hand. He immediately sent news by the next carrier pigeon to his liege King Alfonso II, of the windfall. Recognising a cash cow when he saw one, Alfonso rubber stamped the whole idea and the holy marketing team flogged the idea to the Christians, who being a gullible lot were quick to start flocking in to visit the remains for some salvationist Brownie points.

Hardly CSI standard lab work, but for centuries it has been good enough to attract cashed-up pilgrims to try their luck at redemption in Santiago de Compostela and believers still crowd in today. There really is one born every minute.

In an impressive act of pure faith, as Spain was ravaged with contagious swine flu at the time, Trevor and Jenny departed on their way to get their chunk of heavenly merit, leaving Trish and I to continue the voyage until they could rejoin us.

On a gorgeous morning with not a breath of wind and a mirror surface on the water the two of us prepared to cast off on the journey from Les Onglous to Sète. This would involve crossing the Étang de Thau a large inland salt water lagoon, about 21 km long and 8 km wide and the closest to open water cruising our flat-bottomed inland boat was ever likely to get.

The Étang de Thau is world famous for the shellfish which grow on extensive racks covering a significant proportion of the estuary. Eighteen sorts of shellfish are taken from the area - the most important being oysters. These are marketed under the name of *huîtres de Bouzigues,* after the village where oyster production started. They are a flat variety. Fixed with cement to ropes, the young oysters are immersed in the water until they reach a size suitable for consumption. Thau water is graded A which means that shellfish can be caught and consumed within minutes.

All vessels operating there are governed by strict rules to protect the sensitive environment. Boating charts of the area threaten dire penalties for any toxic discharge into the sacred waters, especially the use of marine toilets.

In accordance with these warnings of dire retribution for disobedience, we set sail well drained and continent to traverse the estuary.

Although the weather was calm when we set out, a stiff breeze slowly started to blow from the east and the surface chop increased, until soon it was blowing over 20 knots with a white capped sea. Challenger One was not designed to handle anything much more than a ripple on a millpond and she rolled around like a drunken barmaid on payday. Kitchen cupboards emptied their contents onto the floor and the library cast itself adrift in the salon, the resulting mix making a sort of *papier-mâché* which slopped from side to side as the boat rolled. Three hours later and without managing to remove any of the oyster beds in passing (though there was one near miss), we were relieved to arrive at Sète and after fortifying ourselves with pastis, began cleaning up the mess.

The modern Sète was built in the middle of the 17th century by the ever industrious Paul Riquet so that his Canal du Midi would have a port on the Mediterranean. The omnipresent Romans were there before him, naming it Mons Setius some 17 centuries earlier, but it was Riquet's new Port-Saint-Louis-du-Cap-de-Cette that became the seaside and canal town of today.

Sète is a really interesting place, like a workaday Venice – lots of canals of varying sizes, loads of small boats tied up in front of buildings lining the canals, a seriously big fishing fleet, cross-Mediterranean ferries, enormous cruise ships, a yacht harbour, water jousting competitions, hustle and bustle.

At Sète, we entered the series of lagoons and canals which become the Canal du Rhône à Sète. This canal follows the Mediterranean coast a couple of kilometres inland and as the name implies it joins Sète with the River Rhône. The canal is surrounded on both sides by shallow marshland and on the way along it we often saw white horses and the black bulls bred for the local 'courses' (bull fights). as well as the occasional pink flamingo which are native to the area.

 The last time I saw pink flamingos I was hallucinating, surfing waves on the green shag pile carpet of my bathroom after a gig with my band, Gerry and the Atrix. It was a night that had involved ingesting a large quantity of toxic substances during our performance. This experience was particularly disturbing as our bathroom doesn't even have carpet, not to mention a flock of Flamingoes, but the little green men riding them seemed friendly, so it seemed okay at the time. Seeing pink flamingoes again also brought back the memory of the subsequent marathon hangover I had next morning. It felt like I was chained to a chair, match sticks propping my eyes open, forced to watch endless synchronised swimming, while someone was banging anvils together inside my head. Something I'd rather not remember, but not as bad as one mistaken fool at the same party who somehow decided a tree was his girlfriend and gave it a ferocious shagging that resulted in the need for some very intimate bandaging.

Frontignan, a picturesque village was our next stop. Here we had to wait until the low bridge was raised vertically on poles which only happens twice each day. Of course when we arrived the bridge was down. Rats! From the guide book it looked like we would have to wait until lunchtime, so we found a place to park up. We asked a fisherman when the bridge would open. "Now!" he said, we looked around and sure enough a section of roadway crossing the canal was levitating into the air to allow a procession of boats to pass underneath it. So much for the official schedule.

Onwards to Palavas les Flots, another Mediterranean holiday resort where streets of tourist shops and cafes line the canal and lead through a picturesque harbour to the sea From our mooring just outside town it was an easy bike ride to the Mediterranean, for a morning of swimming and sun worship.

Coming from Oz where a white pointer is a whacking big shark that eats people, I was immediately impressed by the delightful sight of so many local white pointers. The French penchant for topless sunbathing can only be commended and I was mighty glad I had brought my mirrored sunglasses for hours of discreet talent spotting. The scenery more than compensated for the coarse sand and lack of surf.

The French don't really swim at the beach, they wade in and play ball games, or just stand there looking decorative facing the horizon as if waiting expectantly for a Tsunami that never comes.

After a day at the beach, it was time for some repairs and of course, the washing. A curse of the cruising sailor, is the ongoing need to locate a laundromat. One crew we know doesn't bother. Instead they keep enough clothes to last a month and when they run out, or the pong becomes too great, whichever comes first, they have a giant wash session which takes half a day and pays off the mortgage of the fortunate laundromat owner.

Our weekly wash, means a couple of sackfuls of laundry on the back of the bikes and off for a fascinating morning watching the soap opera of clothes in the tumble dryer. Such is the glamorous and romantic life we pursue.

The density of tourists increases exponentially as one approaches the Mediterranean. Many might consider this a curse, but I think it's great news. After all lets face it, God must have created tourists to be mocked and American tourists doubly so. The way they roam European cities wide eyed, comparing things to their plastic nastiness back home in Ohio, or worse still in Alabama, sets them up for it. The international ignorance engendered in US high schools, by five school semesters of American history to one of world history, fosters comments from Yank tourists like "If this is Austria where are the kangaroos?"

Fortunately, only about 37% of the American population have a passport. This means that nearly 2 out of 3 Americans can't even fly to Canada, let alone travel to anywhere else in the world. Surprisingly, one deterrent to Americans going overseas is cost. A low average income and the high costs associated with raising kids, means that even the cheapest trip abroad would essentially bankrupt a typical US family.

Unfortunately, American culture has now so polluted France with Starbucks, McDonalds and the Euro Disney Theme Park, that maybe in a few years there will be no point for Americans to leave home anyway. Thus I think it is only proper that these cultural vandals should be punished and it is my mission to help the French to do it. Okay, I do realise it's a thin justification, but it works for me.

For years Parisians have enjoyed a largely undeserved reputation for surliness and arrogance towards tourists. Though it's true that the average Parisian is restrained in public and would rather kiss a bubonic monkey than talk to a tourist, they are however, neither unreasonably rude nor unhelpful.

France is the most popular country in the world for tourists and the volume is incredible. If you put yourself in the place of one of the locals and imagine people repeatedly entering your shop and then getting annoyed that you don't speak Russian or Chinese, you have the scenario that many Parisian citizens are faced with daily.   Making even the slightest linguistic effort, even a simple "Bonjour" will suffice and most French people will then do their best to help you on your way.

"Pardon madame, mais je ne parle pas Français", can open the door to hours of amusing charades and fun for the family as you both struggle to make yourselves understood.

But if the French are so friendly, then where did this reputation for being unhelpful to foreigners come from? At last I can reveal the sordid truth, it was probably me! You see I can't help it, it's like a shooting fish in a barrel, American tourists are a larger than life target in life's little shooting gallery of fun and I'm there to go hunting.

It works like this. Chic Parisians in their expensive Chanel and Yves Laurent designer suits, trailing an air of savoir faire and eau de cologne look too daunting for tourists to approach in the street. But enter a rustic old bloke, dressed in a slightly battered leather jacket, goatee beard, and cloth cap and I appear much less daunting to approach and my trap is set.

"Excuse me sir, can you tell me where the Eye-full tower is at?"

As if the baseball cap and plaid shorts weren't enough of a giveaway, that Texas drawl tells me that I've got a live one here.

"Pardon M'sieu, vous êtes Américain?"

'Yessir, how did you know? We're looking for the Eye-full Tower.' He says raising his voice, because volume is well known by Yanks to improve comprehension.

At first Trish used to spoil things at this point when she would butt in and say "Just tell the poor guy." But after a heartfelt discussion about my need to strike a blow against Americanisation, she now leaves me alone and turns away to find the contents of the nearest shop window compelling.

I follow up with polite yet disdainful sentences of heavily accented Gallic. These usually include wayward directions and I have even managed to work the lyrics of the French national anthem into the conversation, until eventually my mark at last wanders off looking dazed and confused.

There are of course variations on this basic theme. As a boat load of Americans were making an erratic attempt to moor their rental boat to a jetty I approached ostensibly to help. Little did they know.

"Donnez moi la corde s'il vous plait msieu, Vite! Vite! Jettez !" my request for them to throw me the mooring rope fell on uncomprehending ears. Perfect!

"La corde M'sieu!" I repeated the call louder and with more emphatic gestures, intended to infer imminent peril and was rewarded with a nervous shout of 'Sorry we don't speak French.'

A frustrated shrug of the shoulders as if to say,

"You poor inferior beings, how do you even manage to get out of bed in the morning?" and I pantomimed throwing the rope. At last they got the idea and once they were secured I approached to enquire if they were American.

"Vous êtes Americain n'est pas? "

"Sorry we don't speak French, mon sewer ,"

"Neither do I, I was just fooling with you."

In fairness it was taken in good humour by some very charming Yanks who enjoyed the joke at their expense and invited me aboard for an evening drinking some very good Bourbon. Who says crime doesn't pay?

I must admit my tourist trolling efforts still require refinement if I am to emulate the genius of an Aussie airline pilot in London. Legend tells how some off duty Qantas pilots were enjoying a few amber libations in a

Soho pub, when a group of Japanese tourists entered following a tweed clad guide carrying a company pennant on high, which her myopic party were following. After a couple of pints of best bitter, the guide felt the need to break the seal and visit the plumbing, so she put her flag down on the bar and disappeared off to the loo. Never one to waste an opportunity, one of the pilots picked up the flag.

"No o tebanasu, Let's go!" he shouted to the visitors and with the standard held high he took off out the front door of the pub. Immediately and without thinking the entire Japanese tour group downed glasses and followed their flag into the street. The pilot led the group on a merry dance through the winding maze of Soho streets, then suddenly ditched the pennant into a bin and ducked up an alley abandoning them. Cockney folklore has it, that the ghosts of those lost Japanese tourists still roam the streets of Soho today. I must lift my game if I am to aspire to such greatness.

I knew an English bloke in Münster, in Germany, who thought he must look particularly Münsterish because people were always asking him for directions in the street. He didn't know the town well and his German was not good but he had worked out a way of coping. He practised the sentence: "Straight ahead two hundred metres, turn left and go to the end of the road. You can't miss it." Thereafter he was able to provide a knowledgeable and confident response to all comers.

Fortunately, the spirit of fair play prevails and it's not all one-way traffic. One young American student we met took his revenge from within, by working for a Parisian cycle tour company.

"Anyone here French, or have French relatives?" he enquired of his guests.

When the answer was invariably negative,"Oh goody" he would say with a smile. 'Because I'm going to take the piss out of these people.' He began with an explanation of how the French invented perfume to

83

cover their own terrible smell, then added gory details of blunt guillotine blades, before subverting the Parisian economy by having his customers stand on their bike seats to peer over the wall of Rodin's sculpture garden, thus avoiding paying the exorbitant entry fee. His hilarious tour exposed the French underbelly and certainly scored many points back for Uncle Sam.

Vive les États Unis! Vive les Touristes!

Bull fights and heavy balls

Le Grau du Roi, is the second largest fishing port in France and the Second World War affected the village profoundly as German troops were stationed there. By 1942, many of the inhabitants had fled, the coast was the front line and bristled with tank traps and minefields. The village was controlled by blockhouses, the canal was blocked to all vessels After Grau du Roi was liberated in August 1944, the coast started to rebuild itself focussing on tourism.

There was not a cloud in the azure blue sky, the day we arrived in Le Grau du Roi to find the canal was again blocked, not by the military, but this time by a procession of boats bedecked with partygoers and flags that was barreling in from the sea towards us. Unbeknownst to us it was the annual Blessing of the Fleet, and we were in a head on confrontation with thirty large commercial trawlers, that were sweeping in from the sea towards us down a narrow channel at a rate of knots. This sort of experience is best described as a quality laxative moment, and thus impelled I made a quick about face and our boat wound up leading the cavalcade through the inner harbour, much to the good humoured amusement of the thousands of spectators on the banks packing the cafes and shellfish restaurants that line the harbour channel all watching the parade.

They cheered our Aussie flag and made lewd comments about the sex lives of Kangaroos as we

85

sailed triumphantly through the outer harbour, under the raised traffic bridge and through the centre of town.

On the fishing trawler behind us the local mayor, a portly gentleman perspiring heavily in his dark suit and tie, but resplendent in his tricolour sash of office, looked perplexed and a bit miffed that his grand moment at the forefront of the flotilla had been usurped by antipodeans in their plastic canal boat, but he took it all in good fun, raised his glass to us and on we motored to the enthusiastic cheers of the locals.

Eventually the convoy made a left turn into the commercial harbour and we stayed to the right in the channel and thus were soon clear of the fishing parade and found the mooring pontoon for visitors. It transpired that this was on the opposite bank to a bull ring. Les Courses were scheduled there later in the afternoon to celebrate the fleet blessing. Fate obviously had intended us to be there, so we sat on the upper deck under the shade of our umbrella sipping Rosé and reading Bullfighting for Dummies, until it was time for the show.

The guide book explained that an indigenous genre of bullfighting is common in the Provence and Languedoc areas, and is known as *Course Camarguaise*. Unlike the cruel Spanish bullfighting in which the bull is physically tortured and killed, the French version is much less bloodthirsty and very entertaining. Fortunately, the traditional brutal Spanish bullfighting which still continues in other parts of France is slowly being legislated out of existence.

Only the French could come up with Course Camarguaise a classic game of advance and retreat and still make it look so stylish. The stars of these spectacles are the bulls, who get top billing and stand to gain fame and statues in their honour, as well as lucrative product endorsement contracts. No longer paraded through the streets to the ring, the bulls are today driven there by truck, after all they are the stars, their names on the posters are written much larger than those of the bullfighters. Camarguaise bullfighting is unique in that the bulls even have a choice not to fight, though most look like they are having a really good time. The object of the contest is for the bullfighter to snatch a rosette from the head of a young bull before the bull has a chance to gore him. The participants, or *Raseteurs*, begin training in their early teens against young bulls from the nearby Camargue region of Provence before graduating to regular contests held principally in Arles and Nîmes, but also in other Provençal and Languedoc towns and villages such as Le Grau du Roi.

By mid afternoon, the stadium was filling with a mixture of locals and tourists. We crossed over the canal on a nearby bridge, then walked past three large statues of charging bulls and bought tickets for the show from a hole in the wall outlet at the stadium.

The building was a light yellow, round concrete amphitheatre with tiered seating. At its centre was a competition ring lined with what appeared to be a mixture of sand, blood and sawdust. The whole thing looked very gladiatorial and a Christians versus Lions match would not have been at all out of the question. I could imagine the commentary.

"A bit of a setback for the home team there, with the loss of their centre apostle, looks like the lions are doing all the preying today, how do you read the score Marcus?"

"That would be Lions three, Christians nil Julius. They're going to need a real miracle to take this one out today."

It was 38 degrees in the shade and no shade, so we joined most of the local crowd taking refuge from the blistering afternoon sun under the bleachers, where concession stands sold food, drinks and kitsch souvenirs. A trumpet fanfare heralded the beginning of the event and we took our seats next to a local family, whose young children were obviously no strangers to this type of entertainment and giggled expectantly as the tension began to build.

Preceding the actual contests, were performances of dancing and horse riding performed by throngs of traditionally clad men and women who first circled the bull ring, before dancing around a giant maypole. The meaning of this seemed completely arbitrary, and I could only hope that it was based on some pagan fertility myth. Next, on came the gladiators dressed all in white, looking like a cricket team who had taken a wrong turn on the way to the MCG. They saluted the crowd, the president of the courses, and the judging panel, then readied themselves for the first bull to be released.

There was a trumpet fanfare and the gates of the arena swung open dramatically revealing the first bovine bulldozer. The massive bull looked peeved at having his daily cow shagging time interrupted by a bunch of cricketers and he leapt over the safety barrier surrounding the ring and cleared out all the competitors who were sheltering there behind it. It looked like he was shelling peas as they all leapt for their lives or swung up into the grandstand to escape five tonnes of high speed hamburger on legs.

Once the bull was coerced back into the ring the real event began. Each bout lasted about 15–20 minutes, during which time the *raseteurs* competed to snatch rosettes tied between the bulls' horns. They didn't take the rosette with their bare hands but rather used a claw-shaped metal instrument called a *raset*. Each *raseteur* worked as a team with a *tourneur* whose job was to distract and taunt the bull into position, so that the *rasteur* could make his run from behind and attempt to collect the ribbons using his claw. Most of the bulls had played this game before and would take off in hot pursuit of the *raseteur*, who to avoid having his insides rearranged by some horn action would leap over the barricade that encircled the ring. At the end of the day the competitor with the highest point score was presented with a trophy and a good time was had by all, including the bulls.

Several days later we ended our dalliance with the Mediterranean. Now that we had reached the River Rhone we could turn north, finally heading in the direction of Paris.

We travelled upriver for days against the opposing current all at the geriatric speed of only five kilometres per hour. Joggers on the shore left us far behind in their wake, thus it was over a week until we reached the beautiful city of Avignon.

The papal court was located in Avignon for most of the fourteenth century and the Pope's Palace and Cathedral form a magnificent group of buildings, but the real fame of Avignon comes from the well known song that has been forever taught to children in schools around the world.

Sur le pont d'Avignon
L'on y danse, l'on y danse
Sur le pont d'Avignon
L'on y danse tous en rond

On the bridge of Avignon
Everyone dances, everyone dances
On the bridge of Avignon
Everyone dances in a circle.

The song dates back to the fifteenth century about a bridge that once crossed the river in Avignon, officially called the Pont St. Bénézet, it is now better known as the Pont d'Avignon on which as the song says, one dances.

Dear reader I was shocked and stunned to discover that the whole thing is a giant myth perpetrated by French language teachers. In what I can only describe as a dastardly plot to misrepresent the facts, I must report several glaring errors in the accepted ballad.

The bridge is a wreck. After being mistreated several times by wars and the flooding Rhône, it was continuously under repair until the seventeenth century, when it ceased to be restored as a lost cause. Now only four arches survive of the original twenty-two and anyone who got too involved with their tango or foxtrot on the remaining span would soon waltz straight off the broken end into the swirling current below. Even ancient health and safety regulations would have not permitted dancing on the bridge. What is even more damming, is that local wisdom reports nobody ever did dance on the bridge. It is believed that the original version of the song was *"Sous le Pont d'Avignon"* (Under the Bridge of Avignon), because in medieval times there were popular cafés with dancing and other wicked pleasure activities on the Ile de la Barthelasse, under the arches of the bridge.

I bring this shameful state of affairs to light, in the hope that any French teachers reading this saga will mend their ways by singing the correct version in future and not corrupt yet another generation of Cherubic innocent scholars.

Trish and I made our personal protest by dancing an enthusiastic but clumsy polka, under the remaining arches. This was much to the amusement of a bus load of Chinese tourists who tried to tell us in sign language, that we had got it all wrong and should pay the €5 entry fee to pirouette on top of the bridge. I pitied these unenlightened souls as they followed their group leaders' flag onto the bridge, little suspecting their role as innocent dupes in the longstanding myth.

Back underway, before long we were leaving the Rhône and entering the River Saône at Lyon, It was with a sense of trepidation that we approached the division of the Rhône and Saône taking the left fork into the city centre. Our guide book warned that the town mooring in Lyon was frequented by low-lifes and one stayed there at personal risk. It was scathing about the port facilities and it warned of junkies, drunks and ne'er do wells hanging around. It was a polite way of saying, moor here and you will get mugged. But we really felt there was time to stop for a few days, and see a little of France's second city. So we decided to chance it.

As we approached the outskirts of the city centre, we spotted a barge on the left bank that had been converted to an *accastillage* or chandlery. A landmark structure and an oasis for river travellers like us, it was a cornucopia of useful things and bits of nauticalia. It is a well known fact amongst boaters, that writing the word marine on an item automatically doubles the selling price even for marine use toilet paper. After some therapeutic retail therapy, involving bits of rope, marine grease and other fabulous stuff, we motored north towards the city centre and our date with destiny and a potential mugging by the local syringe brigade who were reputed to hang out on the quay at our next port of call.

In the city centre on the right bank of the river we found a high stone wall with no street access for a boat such as ours, but set into its stonework was a tap for water, for itinerants such as ourselves and a welcome discovery. Directly opposite on the left bank was the nefarious wharf which looked far from the den of iniquity described by the guide. In fact, it was a beautiful mooring with weeping willow trees, whose branches draped over the moored boats providing very welcome shade from the baking summer sun.

Our lines were taken for us by a neighbouring privateer as we came in to moor and he expressed amazement at our hesitation to land without the reassuring presence of the Gendarmarie. He told us that port Lyon had indeed once deserved the negative press, but it had recently been cleaned up and now was one of the best places to stay on the Saône.

In the afternoon amateur musicians gathered on the quay to practice. These improvised concerts were an absolute delight and covered the whole musical spectrum from jazz to the classics.

That evening as dusk fell, we offloaded our table and chairs and set them up on the quay ready to try out our new BBQ. We had just sat down to share a meal with Simon and Elizabeth the crew of a British boat moored nearby, when a blue and white police patrol car cruised down the quay towards us its blue light flashing. Were we infracting some local by-law?

"Bonsoir M'sieu, un problème?" I said nervously

"Not at all Monsieur, we have just come to wish you *Bon Appétit."* was the courteous reply. The French respect for a good feed, is universal here.

As we finished eating a magnificent dinner the mosquitoes arrived and started tucking into us, so we retired to Simons boat, where I was pleased to see he had a green spiral mosquito coil hanging in the cabin in readiness for our arrival.

"Great things those aren't they? Though I find the smell they make when they burn a bit strong,"

Simon just looked stunned, the blank look on his face made me wonder what I'd said. Elizabeth doubled over with laughter, tears of mirth were running down her cheeks. When she could finally speak again she said,

"We couldn't understand the French instructions, other than the bit about good for eight hours, so Simon has been hanging them up for eight hours then chucking them away, we never knew you were supposed to burn them."

Simon slunk away looking rather sheepish and I felt a bit sorry for him for a nano second, but he recovered well aided by an rejuvenating glass of Beaujolais.

That was not the only linguistic catastrophe that was to mark our sojourn in Lyon.

The following night Simon and Elizabeth joined us for dinner in the delightful food quarter of the city. For several centuries Lyon has been known as the French capital of gastronomy, due in part to the presence of many of France's finest chefs as well as two of France's best known wine-growing regions being located near Lyon. The Beaujolais is to the North, and the Côtes du Rhône is to the South.

Lyon is the home of very traditional restaurants known as *bouchons* serving local dishes and local wines. The restaurant area on the West bank is packed with these as well as the usual cafes and bistros and we could see that we were in for a culinary treat.

After a careful inspection of the establishments we chose a Á La Traboule which had a sticker showing the marionette Gnafron, a Lyonnais symbol of the pleasures of dining, with a glass of wine in one hand and a napkin bearing the Lyon crest in the other identifying the establishment as one of Les Authentiques Bouchons Lyonnais

Elizabeth is allergic to certain food chemicals thus has to be very careful of what she orders. And with very limited French at her disposal this can be a challenge sometimes.

"Monsieur, je suis trés allergique aux preservatifs", She said to the waiter. Imagine her reaction when the waiter broke out into fits of laughter as did the locals at the adjacent tables.

'What did I say?' quizzed Liz.

'Liz my dear, a *préservatif* is the French word for a condom and the establishment are understandably very sad to hear of your allergy to them." I managed to splutter through my own laughter. This time it was Richards turn to guffaw, as Elizabeths' face turned a thermometer shade of red with embarrassment.

Our dinners of Salade Lyonnaise, Foie de veau persillé followed by Tarte Praline were washed down with a couple of litres of local Côtes du Rhône, which did not disappoint and it was a well contented merry band of sailors who cackled their way back to the port that night.

Next morning it was time for a for a bit of touristing. The Basilica de Notre Dame at Lyon has wonderful mosaics walls, floors and ceilings, the most recent of which is a huge wall fresco by a Ukraine artist in 2004, depicting the pilgrim paths through France into Spain. At the sight of this I couldn't help but wonder how Trevor and Jenny had got on with St Jimmy the Fish in Santiago de Compostela? A couple of late conversions for Saint James perhaps, to add to his dubious legend?

Trish and I explored the famous *Traboules*, the intricate network of passages and tunnels that run throughout the old city. These were originally constructed in the fourth century to allow the silk merchants to transport their wares throughout the city, without getting them wet. In the Second World War the *Traboules* many of which were little known or undocumented in city records, became a refuge for freedom fighters of the resistance which was nationally based in Lyon.

The city was also the home to the tragic story of French hero Jean Moulin, who was tasked with uniting the warring factions of the resistance. In 1943 the different factions of the Resistance were doing more damage to themselves than to the occupying Germans with each group jockeying for political position, to the point of betraying rival countrymen to the Nazis. Jean Moulin was sent by the Gaullist forces in London to get them to remove their digits and focus on the real enemy. After some initial success Jean was betrayed to the infamous Butcher of Lyon, Klaus Barbie and he came to a sticky end at the hands of the Gestapo. It is unknown who betrayed him as well as several other principals of the Resistance to the Germans and the conspiracy theories continue to this day. Nowadays the headquarters of the Gestapo in Lyon is a museum

94

dedicated to the brave men and women of the French resistance.

Where better in France than Lyon to learn to play the national bowling game of Pétanque or boule. *Boule lyonnaise* - is probably the oldest of the French boules sports. The current version of the game developed during the eighteenth century around the area of Lyon. The casual form of the game of pétanque is today played by about 17 million people in France, mostly during their summer vacations. It is very popular and may be seen played in any open space in villages and towns, with people of all ages lobbing small cannonballs in all directions. In larger cities such as Paris it is played along the Champ-de-Mars esplanade under the trees on each side.
A glass of wine and a hand full of balls, what's not to love?

HOW TO PLAY PÉTANQUE DOUBLES
Pétanque the more commonly played game, is a form of boules where the goal is, while standing with the feet together in a circle, to throw metal balls close to a small wooden ball called a *cochonnet*, or little piglet. The game is normally played on hard dirt or gravel, but can also be played on grass, sand or other surfaces. Boules is more complicated than it appears. Most teams will have a player who specialises in the lob. Basically a high drop shot that aims to blast opponents away from the jack whilst other players focus more on getting close to the *cochonnet*. You will need:

Four people
Three boules per person
One white ball (*The cochonnet*)

Toss a coin (preferably double headed) to decide which team will start the game.

Play starts by the toss winner drawing a circle roughly 50cm diameter somewhere on the terrain (Playing field) Standing inside the circle the first player throws the Jack between 6-10 meters in any direction.

The team that won the toss also throws the first boule aiming to land as close to the Jack as possible.

From here on the team that does not have the closest boule to the Jack is the team that throws next. This team continues to throw until they get a ball closer to the *cochonet* or they run out of boules.

Play ends when all balls have been thrown.

Points are scored for the winning team with the closest boule only.

E.g. if team A has the closest two balls to the Jack, that would score two points. If they only have the closest ball to the Jack and Team B is second closest then that is a score of one point for team A. Team B doesn't score.

The match ends and is won by the first team to 11 points.

Bon Chance

Salad Lyonnaise

2 tablespoons olive oil
1 tablespoon butter
1 garlic clove, finely chopped
1/2 baguette, cut into cubes
  Fine sea salt
  Freshly ground black pepper
4 strips bacon
1 tablespoon white-wine vinegar
1 teaspoon Dijon mustard
4 large eggs
1 teaspoon white vinegar
8 ounces frisée, torn into pieces.

1. To make croutons, warm 1 tablespoon olive oil and butter in a sauté pan set over medium heat. Add garlic and cook for 1 minute. Add cubed bread and toast, tossing often, until brown and crisp, about 5 minutes. Season with salt and pepper.
2. Wipe out pan and return to medium-high heat. Add bacon and cook until all fat has rendered and bacon is crisp. Remove bacon to plate. Reserve remaining fat in the pan.
3. Crack each egg into an individual ramekin. Prepare a bowl of ice water.
4. Bring a shallow saucepan with 3 inches of water and white vinegar to a boil. Reduce to a simmer. Once large bubbles have subsided and only small bubbles remain, carefully slide each egg into pan with ramekin placed close to the surface of the water. Poach 2 eggs at a time for 3 to 4 minutes. Using a slotted spoon, remove eggs to ice water.
5. In large bowl make the vinaigrette by whisking together 2 tablespoons olive oil, 1 tablespoon reserved bacon fat, white-wine vinegar, and mustard. Season with salt and pepper. Add frisée and toss to coat.

6. Divide the greens among four plates. Top each salad with croutons. Crumble 1 strip bacon per plate. Carefully remove eggs from water bath and blot with a paper towel. Remove any lacy edges. Place 1 egg on top of each salad and sprinkle with salt and pepper. Serve immediately. Yield: 4 appetizer servings.

Bon Appetit

A day in the life of a gutter crawler

0730 Woke up and looked at my watch. Darn thing had stopped again, it hasn't been the same since it got filled up with water SCUBA diving in Croatia. So much for it being water resistant. Not to worry, no deadlines to keep and Trish was still asleep anyway, so I rolled over under the covers and pretended the day had yet to dawn. ZZZZZZ

0815 We are moored to a floating dock with power and water, so I decided to get out of bed and wash down the boat. Trish stirred and said she wanted to do that job, so I got up and started demolishing the front bathroom, to remove the toilet which was swinging loose. We first discovered a problem when one of our guests capsized off the loo as the floor gave way from under her. Chronic water leakage from the adjacent shower had rotted away the support of the toilet bowl, so all the cabinetry has to be removed and much of it replaced. Pretty soon I have chunks of rotten wood flying in all directions and the front half of the boat looks like a demolition yard.

This also is our only non electric loo and the morning pumping has never been popular with the occupants of the front cabin. We have three toilets, possibly because it's an ex rental boat, but maybe the English designers had an incontinence problem. This is a great opportunity to get rid of the pump out bowl and upgrade to an electric crapper.

While Trish scrubs the decks I cut up the old loo floor panels and dispose of them in a nearby dockside bin. I get a friendly bonjour from the local council worker as he waters the flower boxes on the quay. Most French villages are a part of the program called *Fleurissement de France* in which both private citizens and town councils place and maintain flower boxes of colourful blooms throughout their towns, just for the beautification of their environment. This is very a successful concept and is a highlight of French summer. Onboard to keep up with the locals we even have a tame Geranium named Phoebe on deck and four flower boxes full of fresh herbs hang from the guard rails.

0900 Michael, a new acquaintance from the adjacently moored English yacht ACAPELLA, drops by to tell us he has phoned a friend who is cruising ahead upstream on the river Saône and he gives us the latest advice on whom to contact for repairs when we eventually reach St Jean De Losne. We canalliers are very helpful to each other in sharing information about ports, prices, restaurants, local wines and the other essentials of boating life, like Internet access and where to fill with water and fuel. We are an independent community and boat ownership is the certificate of membership.

It is surprising how many floating gypsies there are here in France, I have so far identified three classes of boating citizens. There are the casual renters, here for short stay holidays, that we refer to as Bumpers, because of their tendency to bounce their boats in and out of locks due to an excess of enthusiasm and a lack of experience. These people are a holiday crowd out for maximum fun per day, so they are always lively, good for a drink and a story at all hours.

Secondly there are The Regulars, fair weather summer season only boat owners like us. Our boats are identified by multiple flower boxes, individual boat names and skippers who do not adopt kamikaze techniques of lock entry at full speed favoured by the less experienced. We choose instead to guard our precious paintwork by entering slowly and with a minimum of fuss.

Finally, there are the hard core crowd, The Liveabords who dwell on their boats all year round rain or shine. They often own large, beautifully decorated ex-commercial barges of 20 metres or more. These guys cluster in three main ports over the winter season to hibernate and entertain each other with social nights and dinner parties to while away the long cold nights. Not a way to live for the faint hearted or thermally challenged.

0930 Breakfast. Couldn't be bothered walking to the *boulangerie* for croissants today, so it's Muesli and *Yaourt*. (Yoghurt)

1000 We decide that we probably ought to do something today and will get underway and head towards Mâcon. After medicinal coffee, we cast off and with a following wind, head north. Not much adverse current today in the river Saône so we make good time. Although our hull is 14 metres long, with only a small 57 horsepower motor hurrying is never an option. This lack of power does mean that we have to check river currents before embarking on the main stream. If the downstream current is very fast after winter snow melts, or if the upstream hydroelectric dams are releasing too much water, we may just have to wait for things to slow down a bit. In flood periods, friends have had to wait weeks on some rivers before being able to proceed.

The rivers we have traveled so far have been wonderfully free of annoying noisy speedboats and jet skis. Commercial boats overtake us traveling much

101

faster, but in general other craft travel at our leisurely pace.

What wonderful countryside this is, the Beaujolais vineyards are on my left so I know what wine we shall be having with dinner tonight. Tall trees and farmland are on the right. Every now and then a commercial barge passes loaded with building sand.

1115 More coffee. Whilst I steer on the fly bridge, Trish has been having a mending day in the main cabin. She has sewn up two of my T shirts and is now repairing the hem of the table cloth. The boat carries on up river.

1230 We arrive at the first and only lock we will encounter today, Red light! No entry.

Most locks have a traffic light system to tell you when to enter them. Red is No go. Red and Green: Get ready to Enter. Green: Come on in. Double red: lock is broken call the *éclusier* from the VNF.

We have hit a red light so we tie up at a nearby jetty and wait for our turn. Although it is possible to radio or telephone the lock keeper and ask how long the wait will be, we never bother, we are not in a hurry, it doesn't matter to us if we have to wait.

Whilst Trish keeps an eye on the lock lights I duck below for a shower. The engine heats the water and we have an excellent shower system

1300 Green light. At last we enter the lock.

This particular lock is a concrete chasm about 200 metres long. We are heading upstream and the basin is empty so we have the whole massive space to ourselves and we tie up to a wall on the port side. Behind us the huge metal gates close, then water starts flooding in.

Imagine filling ten Olympic swimming pools in ten minutes and you get some idea of the water flow. Trish is controlling the length of the mooring rope pulling in

102

the slack as we go up and I use the motor to keep us from swinging away from the lock wall as rushing water swirls around us. Eventually, we are at the top and the gates open to let us out.

1400 Lunch time. Fresh baguette with tuna and salad. More Coffee. All eaten whilst underway towards Mâcon. Download email. We have a French USB internet modem which allows us to access the internet from the boat. This is expensive so for long sessions or to talk on SKYPE, we either find a local library, or go to McDonalds. Almost all McDonalds in France have free Wi Fi. On rainy days we have spent whole mornings with Ronald, logged on to the interweb just for the price of a coffee.

1500 We arrive at Mâcon a town of 40,000 people. We pass by the commercial harbours moving fast now, with a very strong tail wind blowing about 18 knots. The first visitors jetty is full of boats. Damn. Further along the second and third town jetties are full as well. Though most of these people have just stopped for lunch, it leaves us with nowhere to go. Rafting up alongside another boat whilst permitted is unpopular in France. If a heavily loaded commercial barge should pass, its bow wave may cause considerable damage if the rafted vessels bounce heavily against each other and the stonework of the quay.

1600 Having passed through Mâcon town our last hope of a mooring is the Port de Plaisance on the outskirts. As we enter, the Port captain hails and directs us to where he wants us to tie up. He wants me to reverse the boat into a space less than the width of my boat and moor to the jetty stern to. This is a major challenge as we only have a single propeller thus steering in reverse is very difficult for a 46 foot boat. Added to this there is a 15 knot cross wind. It takes me three attempts, but eventually we are safely moored and enjoying a joke with the captain. The conversation is the usual Franglais, a half and half mixture of my French and his English. We enjoy a good laugh when he says his guest computer doesn't have an entry category for Australians, most of his clients are French, Dutch or English. We make it clear that we are not to be entered as English, so he puts us down as Austrian. Fair enough!

1620 We off-load the bikes and cycle three kilometres into the centre of Mâcon for a look around. Not a particularly interesting town, but it is in the last weeks of their summer sales. Unlike Australia where every week is a sale, France has rules about this. Shops are only allowed to advertise sales for a limited time and so they radically mark down things in price. I buy a new T shirt for only €5 and Trish buys clothes for our granddaughter at throw away prices.
While Trish continues shopping I cycle about 5 kilometres to find a hardware store. Unfortunately, they don't have a suitable colour laminate for the new bathroom floor so I return to the boat empty handed.

1800 Typing at the computer before dinner. Check the programs on satellite TV.

2100 Dinner.   It is Trish's night off cooking tonight. I make a small vinaigrette salad followed by Herbed Chicken and vegetables accompanied by a Côte du Rhone Rose purchased locally at the vineyard when we passed through Avignon.
 We check the weather forecast for tomorrow on TV. It's going to be hot again, 34 degrees. We discuss tomorrow's destination and agree to head for the picturesque town of Tournus.

2130 TV time. We have a choice of movies onboard. The iPod, Movies downloaded on the computer. Free to air French TV, or we even have a satellite dish that gets over 200 channels. It's ridiculous really this is more computer technology than was used to send man to the Moon.

Decided to watch the Year in Tibet BBC series on BBC4

2300 Nodded off in front of the TV. Trish is reading in bed. Just before lights out Trish gets a call on her French mobile. Wrong number. Two minutes later an insistent French woman calls back and is telling Trish that there must be a Camille on this number, as it is inconceivable she has made a mistake. Trish manages to persuade her that perhaps her friend has given her the wrong number, no easy feat when you consider the vocabulary involved. We have improved vastly with our French, but everyday conversation is still a challenge.

2310 Horizontally happy in bed. Each day on the inland waterways is different, each bend in the river and new village is a feast of discovery with new sights, history, foods and people. Tomorrow we shall again set a course north for our next stop on the journey to Paris. Who knows what will happen next?

ZZZZZZZZZZZZZZZZZZZZZZZZZZZZZZZZZZZZZZZZZ
ZZZZZZZZZ

I love nature because it beats having to flush

Jarod Kintz

Ships log: River Saône Northbound   July

In case you are getting the idea that our voyage was all sweetness and light traveling through the magic fairyland of France, I should point out at this juncture that there was a dark side too. It didn't raise its ugly head very often, but when it did, it was all the more striking by contrast. *Merde* happens!

Though the small villages we passed through, like country towns everywhere were almost crime free, there was never an absolute guarantee of safety from mischief. Occasionally a boat would be cast adrift at night by some young stirrer who decided to untie the mooring lines. Usually this would be no big deal, the boat might drift over the other side of the canal, but couldn't go far in real terms. However, one unfortunate couple we met were woken by urgent cries from a fisherman on the bank and came on deck to find themselves drifting towards a weir. It was only thanks to the fisherman's timely warning that they woke in time to save the boat. They now padlock the boat to something secure whenever possible at night and we follow their example.

So far we had experienced no such trouble on Challenger One, but later we did have a spot of aggravation with the locals on a couple of occasions.

The first happened at a small marina on the Nivernais canal. We were all snugged up in bed for the night when a knock came on the door just as we were nodding off to sleep. It was the harbourmaster demanding the mooring fee. I staggered out of bed none too impressed at being disturbed and after explaining to him that this was not an appropriate time of day, paid the charge and went back to bed

The mooring fee included showers and toilet facilities, both of which remained locked and inaccessible all day. We also heard from an adjacent boat that we had been overcharged.

Trevor, who had now returned from his pilgrimage in Spain a holier and slimmer man, agreed with me that the next time this bloke came in the middle of the night for his fee we'd get out of our respective beds where we sleep *au naturel*, give him the Full Monty and tell him where he could stick his fee and how many turns he should rotate it when it got there.

Sure enough the following night at ten o'clock there was another knock on the door. I leapt out of bed, but not wanting to intimidate the bloke with my huge willy, wrapped on a towel and jumped onto the dock to confront him. In French I explained to him that his behaviour was not acceptable and anyway the facilities were not available, being locked up half the day and that he had a cheek expecting us to pay. The harbourmaster gave me a heated reply that this was the most convenient time for him to call. One thing lead to another and soon fists were being shaken and tempers were rising. Meanwhile, Trevor bless his soul, had appeared on deck starkers as promised to lend moral support, but as he sensed that this conflict was about to lead to biffo, he retreated momentarily to his cabin to put on some battle shorts before the fists started flying.

While he was below I had an epiphany, and realised that I was having a good old shouting match all in French, complete with effusive Gallic hand gestures and was rather enjoying myself. Slowly the tide of the conversation turned, tempers cooled and we sorted out what was really just a misunderstanding. Apparently, the shower block was available, we just had to collect a key, which nobody had thought to tell us about. The mooring cost varied with length of the boat and Monsieur reluctantly agreed not come so late in future to collect his fee.

This seemed all very agreeable and by the time Trevor got back on deck properly attired for a punch up, we were shaking hands amicably and were now the best of friends.

Next morning my new mate Gaston and I were on excellent terms, we exchanged greetings with a smile and the grand fracas and nocturnal naked confrontation was all forgotten.

I am not naturally pugnacious, but the other event that nearly led to blows happened in Saverne. After a long hot day of travel, we arrived late at the marina to find the moorings were all full. Closer inspection revealed there was one last free space, which would require some very tricky manoeuvring in reverse to get the boat into a spot between two other large boats with our stern on the pontoon. After much shunting, I managed to get the boat secured and all I wanted was a shower, a beer and a nap, but first I had to connect the electricity. Jumping off the boat onto the pontoon I discovered that all the power sockets were taken. Buggeration! To solve the problem I pulled a plug, put in a double adapter and returned both leads to share the socket. That was my big mistake.

The next thing I knew an irate, huge hairy-chested bloke was storming off his boat towards me waving his arms angrily. He had long blond hair, a long droopy blond moustache, muscles on his muscles and without a word of exaggeration, if this wasn't Hulk Hogan the wrestler, it had to be his twin brother. The bloke was really pissed off, how dare I unplug his lead, I had crashed his computer and had ruined his life. He ripped out my plug and wouldn't hear a word of my attempts to apologise.

From the pulsing of his temporal blood vessels and the steam coming out of his ears I thought he was going to clock me for sure. However, with his fury vented he returned to his boat where he continued to stare enough daggers at our boat that I thought they would sink us.

Next morning as I walked down the jetty past the Hulk, I wished him Bonjour. He just glowered, though his wife disloyally nodded and returned my greeting.

Fortunately, that day he set sail and so I put the incident out of my mind.

Two days later as we approached our mooring for the evening, there was again only one space left. Oh no! It was right next to Hulk Hogans' boat. There was nothing for it but to tie up and wear the pain. I greeted the Hogans and received a smile from Madame and a cursory dismissive nod from the Hulk, who was clearly not impressed that the saboteur was following him.

For the next few days we enjoyed cruising up the River Sarre arriving in the beautiful town of Metz in time for the Mirabelle season. This delicious little yellow plum can be used in so many creative ways, from jams to wine to moon rockets. As I approached the pontoon, there he was again, Hulk Hogan and you guessed it, the only space was right next to him.

Next morning my "kill him with kindness," campaign was starting to get results. My smiling morning bonjour, which I made sure he couldn't ignore, now received a monosyllabic grunt from the monarch of the wrestlers.

A week later the feud forgotten we cruised towards Toul and decided to stop in a secluded bay off the side of the river? A small lagoon with only enough room for two boats and one space was already occupied. Surely not... Of all the boats in France, it was my nemesis, Hulk Hogan. That evening I had a long chat with Mrs Hulk, whilst Hogan sat nearby silent, listening and

109

picking his teeth, as if to ignore my existence, though I sensed my presence was now producing less smoke and steam.

Next port we again shared a jetty, but this time Hulk had to talk to me when I asked him about power supplies on the unattended jetty. He didn't jump down my throat, but merely said he had been unable to locate the harbourmaster to ask for permission. I plugged in anyway.

Our final encounter was a week later in Liverdun as we arrived, almost predictably, there was the Hulks boat secured to the sole pontoon jetty. What a change, this time he emerged from his boat to welcome us and take our lines. Could this be the same fellow who had nearly ripped my head off and pissed down my neck? As the season was ending I asked where he was going to spend winter and he explained that he was heading south to St Jean de Losne and so this would be our parting of the ways, but he hoped that we would meet again next year, he introduced himself and his wife and we shook hands and exchanged boat cards and parted the best of friends. With any luck our paths will cross again next year. Alain and Claudia wherever you are I salute you *mes amis* and I will never touch your plug ever again.

Not every cruising day smells of roses, occasionally things just spontaneously turn to crap. Every boatie has a toilet story and I think it only fair and in the interest of balanced reporting that I should share a tale of ours. I give fair warning that this *histoire* is a bit on the nose and those with a squeamish olfactory disposition may wish to fast forward to the next chapter. One of the many wonderful things about cruising is the autonomy. A boat is a self-contained dwelling with its own water, gas and electricity supplies as well as its own sewerage system, all of which must be nurtured and sustained to ensure they continue to function. No city council is there to pander to the needs of the

110

privateer when the power goes out, or the water runs dry, but equally there are no escalating utility bills arriving weekly in the mailbox either. It would be impressive if they did, as we haven't even got a letter box.

Constant vigilance is required which means that most of the time they all work fine. True, on occasion we have had to resort to buckets of water for drinking supplies when the pump decided to take a vacation. Another time candles were essential for a week and added a certain renaissance charm, when the batteries gave out.   Overall these minor inconveniences are a small price to pay for the freedom we enjoy as gutter crawling gypsies.

Unfortunately, most boats have the sewerage system of a medieval castle, i.e. if it smells bad, bung it out the window or overboard.   Challenger One arrived with three separate toilets as a legacy of her charter days when the tour operators squeezed as many souls as possible aboard to justify their high rental charges.

To use the correct terminology, nautical types refer to toilets as "the heads," from the old sailing ship days when sailors hung their bums over the side of the bow near the ships figurehead. Presumably all those figure heads of semi clad nymphs were to cheer the lads up mid performance. Quite a good idea really, but I haven't had much success persuading Trish that our loo needs a bit of soft porn in the bogs to help me pass the time. That's one motion that has failed to pass.

Fortunately, there is none of that rag and string sailboating on our ship, we travel strictly by the burning of noxious oil and so I feel quite safe calling a Crapper, a Crapper. Two of ours are long drops. You can look down the hole, target a passing fish and then drop the kids off at the pool. Yes, that's right, it goes straight into the canal. This always seems to upset sensitive types who then picture the canals as one huge open sewer. Nothing could be further from the truth, as the volume of water in the 11,000 kilometres of canals handles a bit of organic fertiliser with no trouble at all. This all very bio-friendly really, but does rather put one off fishing.

The green colour of the canal water comes not from nasties, but from all the vegetable matter on the bottom. Canal banks are kept mowed and all the cuttings go straight in the canals, as do the leaves of the overhanging deciduous trees. All this compost requires periodic dredging, or emptying of the canals to maintain the proper depth. So the long drop toilets are no problem and there is really nothing to go wrong with a hole in the bottom of the boat.

The third toilet we inherited was a pump out variety toilet. These are very popular in sailboats with the yachtie crowd, who seem to think there is something organically natural about beating to windward, heeling over at an angle under sail, holding on to the bogs for dear life, whilst pumping to flush and empty the bowl These dunnies have been around since the late 1800's but tend to block easily when inexperienced guests ignore warnings and insist on stuffing them full of enough tissue to wallpaper a mansion.

This leads me to a discussion of how much paper is really enough. Some people just don't seem to feel the paperwork is done properly unless they go through half a roll of toilet paper. Those of you with children, will know that it seems to take enough paper to fill an encyclopaedia at each performance and bulk toilet rolls feature in every weekly supermarket trip.

My Dad always talked fondly of his days in the British Army, where each man was issued with three sheets of army form blank each day for toilet paper, need it or not. The instructions were, one piece for wipe up, one for wipe down and one to polish. What more do you need? He was however prepared to admit, that army training manuals were often put to better supplemental use in the latrine block by those not prepared to adhere strictly to these rules.

112

Back on-board all was going well with our loos, until one morning after his regular ablutions in the pump out loo, Trevor, who is keen on sharing all information, said, "I think either the world just shook for me, or the dunny is starting to move."

On examination I found that he was right. The floor under the toilet was starting to give way, so the bowl was starting to wobble precariously and it was only a matter of time before there was a disastrous capsize mid-performance.

There was nothing for it but the rotten floor under the toilet would have to be removed and the whole plinth on which it stood be replaced with a new one and an electric loo.

It took a few days but when it was finished it looked splendid. Because of the holding tank below, the bowl sat on an elevated plinth like a royal throne and ones legs dangled in mid-air when enthroned. By the left hand side the new power buttons were ready to operate the electric mechanism that replaced the pump. The whole thing was magnificent and for reasons that will soon become evident, Trevor christened it the Shredder.

The Shredder worked fantastically, it was just like a normal domestic appliance. No more frantic hand pumping, but because it was a macerator as well, it was very noisy. Some said it was like the ruckus made by an angry Terrier protecting the virtue of an aged dowager, though I reckoned it sounded more like a jet engine inhaling a flock of very surprised and unhappy seagulls.

The noise made by the Shredder proved very unpopular with people who's sensitivities apparently precluded making public the knowledge that they actually went for number twos. With the Shredder, privacy was a thing of the past, everyone knew who was doing what, in real time.

Trevor on the other hand bonded with the Shredder and took great delight regaling us with the DAILY SHREDDER REPORT at breakfast. Each morning he recounted in detail his personal challenge to the machinery and how again the Shredder had overcome even the most objectionable parts of his previous night's diet. Nothing seemed to daunt the Shredder and life was good.

This happy state of affairs with the new fangled Shredder continued until one day the presence of guests aboard forced Trevor to vacate his bathroom of choice and move to the rear facilities. These were very boring in comparison and there were no more daily reports for the duration of their stay. Trevor was magnanimous in relinquishing his exclusive throne and was careful to brief the guests on the virtues of the Shredder and its proper diet, but he warned them not to feed it too generously with paper for fear of giving it indigestion.

Lying in bed one morning at the other end of the boat Trevor heard the Shredder start its morning song which suddenly came to a strangled note and stopped. Oh no! Someone had stuffed the Shredder. Repeatedly the guilty party tried to get the Shredder to clear the blockage. Each time the Shredder tried valiantly to munch itself through the telephone book wad of paper in its throat and then jammed. Trevor lay in his bunk thinking

"I bloody well warned them what would happen. My poor Shredder is suffering and I'm not moving to fix it."

After twenty minutes of futile efforts all of a sudden the Shredder screamed back into action. It had overcome the blockage. What a relief that was?

Next time but with a different guest and who had also ignored the warning it all happened again. This time it was too much for the poor Shredder, the thrombosis was terminal and nothing would shift the blockage. That

114

meant that it was up to Captain Muggins to fix it. Moi!
Oh *Merde*!

I could tell that working in the confined poorly ventilated
bathroom was not going to be pleasant. Perhaps it
would be easier to sell the boat? Eventually, I sent
everybody ashore and in true Captain Scott fashion
said, "I may be some time."

I'll spare you the gory details, suffice it to say I had to
dismantle the entire apparatus to reach the stoppage
and was up to my ankles in brown foul smelling guano.
It was the most nauseating job I have ever had to
undertake and a few times I came close to losing my
lunch. Two hours later when the crew returned, I was
able to report success, but swore I would never do that
again. Ever!

A month later the emotional scars of the experience
had almost faded when it did happen again. In spite of
dire warnings to all comers and the threat that he or
she who blocked the Shredder, cleans the Shredder,
another set of guests managed to choke it.

Let's call the offender Alice (Because that's her name),
she beat an embarrassed retreat ashore whilst her
husband Bob, a beefy Queenslander, gamely offered to
do the deed, bless his heart. Bob has the manual
dexterity of a dyslexic baboon in boxing gloves, so
there was nothing for it but to take on the foul task
myself.

This time I knew what I was in for and it called for
serious preparation, so I got roaring drunk. It was the
only way I could pre-medicate myself to approach that
horrible job again. Of course it took a little while for the
medicine to adequately numb my senses, so while I
waited I gave the whole problem a little thought with the
few remaining brain cells not too pickled to synapse.
What if I could give the Shredder an enema instead of
dismantling it? Perhaps a good purgative would do the
job and save me much grief and mess.

As the half bottle of Pernod I had swallowed kicked in I decided that I was probably smashed enough to begin. I would try the enema. I crammed a hosepipe down the Shredders throat and shouted to shore for Trish to turn on the water tap, then I pressed the toilet flush button. The Shredder coughed twice, went quiet, then let out a mighty roar as the douche blasted the blockage through and the electric motor roared back into action, the problem was solved.

I think I was even more relieved at not having dismantle the whole apparatus again than the Shredder was. Being already three sheets to the wind, it was only right to toast the happy moment, so that is what I did and then passed out a happy man.

Boat toilets. Bah!

I went down to the crossroads......

Robert Johnson

In the warm summer sunshine it was easy cruising from Lyon northwards on the river Saône. The river was wide and although there was some large commercial traffic that loomed above us as they overtook, there was plenty of room for everyone to pass by safely. The river banks whose height changes dynamically with the amount of water flowing downstream, were too shallow for us to approach, each day we covered long distances between the harbours where we could tie up and stop for the night. There were also many cruise ships plying the river with their elderly overfed passengers taken off by waiting buses at each halt, to be shown the local highlights before being returned safely to their palaces for an afternoon nap and even more gourmet food. Every waterway should have cruise ships like these, giant black holes that suck in precisely the sort of people that we want to avoid. Brilliant.

Though we were motoring upstream, the downstream current was small and so each day saw good northward progress, at last the voyage seemed to be going smoothly, but all that was about to change.

At this time of year the days are long and hot with the sun still lights the sky until almost ten in the evening. Anchoring out of the marked channel was likely to be risky. If the pick dragged during the night, we would find ourselves a sitting duck in the middle of the commercial

117

channel in the path of the massive barges that travel through the night. So it was relief after one long day underway and with darkness about to descend, that we moored for evening in the centre of the town of Tournus, at a pontoon jetty next to a road, shaded by beautiful plane trees.

Night fell and we had just finished dinner, when a council van arrived and started setting off explosives to frighten the birds out of those same plane trees. Thousands of small birds took flight as firecrackers detonated below. They rose into the air to be silhouetted like a dark cape against the night sky. I thought they must be starlings and their numbers were astounding. I discovered later that the explosions were intended to frighten them away from the immediate area, which is a big grape growing region and have them continue their migration south, to become a problem for someone else.

Next morning I had an unrelated brainwave. Perhaps I was jolted from my comfort zone by the fireworks of the previous night.

'Let's get a second steering position upstairs,' I said to no one in particular. There was no connection between the two matters that I could make, it was just a sudden idea that had bubbled to the surface in a sort of light bulb moment.

The helming position inside the main cabin was fine on cold and rainy days, but now that the sun had decided to come out and play on a regular basis, steering inside the cabin had become quite unpleasant. Both the hot summer air and the heat of Brutus the noisy engine, made the saloon's temperature unbearable and this was sucking some of the fun out of the cruise.

We watched with envy as other boats motored past with their crews sitting on deck in the sunshine, where they were enjoying the panoramic views, uninterrupted by cabin windows. It was so pleasant outside, that we had been taking turns to go below to steer rather than expiring in the airless cabin below.

As I ran the idea of transforming the boat through my head, it occurred to me that there was a safety consideration here as well. From the inside wheel when entering locks, it was impossible to see Trish on the stern readying the mooring rope. She could easily fall in, with me none the wiser and the risk of losing her cheerfulness and culinary expertise would be a tragedy of epic proportions. Where else could I find someone to put up with me, at short, or even long notice?

There was plenty of aft deck room, adding a steering station outside sounded such a brilliant idea, that we resolved to do it. How hard could it be? A bit of control wire, a new shiny steering wheel, perhaps half a days work to connect it all up and then Bob's your uncle, the panorama of rooftop views would be ours. If only I could have known we were about to begin a task, that would make Hannibal's elephant trek across the Alps, look like a stroll in the park with a poodle, I might have not done it.

Of course the majority of shipwright businesses capable of doing the work, were now far behind us on the Mediterranean coast. Locating a marine mechanic inland, looked like it would might be as hard as finding a surf shop at Ayers Rock.

Chatting with other mariners we learned that in the centre of France, in the heart of the Burgundy region, about 25 km southeast of Dijon was a small town reputed to be able to help.

St Jean de Losne, is both the crossroads of the French canal system and the biggest pleasure boat harbour in France. Everything at Saint Jean de Losne is about barging, there are pieces of boats everywhere. This is one of the capitals of the barging world, a place where you can find any type of engine part for any engine, from Boudin to Volvo. There are some of the most skilled marine welders available and mechanics said to live and breathe DAF, Perkins and Scania diesel fumes. Here canal dwellers will find everything they need, from dry docks for commercial barges, to fenders and even those really twee Greek fishermen's caps that spell out "Wanker below."

The town of Saint Jean is a very active place of passage, people and barges that come and go all year round, it is a wonderful location to meet others and share barging experiences. In the centre of the town there is even a museum dedicated to the history of the inland waterways and on the floor above it is a free library, where English speaking boaters meet twice weekly to exchange both books and information.

Charming though it is, St Jean is a working town, if you remain there it is because there is something wrong with your barge or boat. There are several repair yards in St Jean and nearby St Usage, both with their passionate advocates and detractors. One thing everybody we spoke to did agree upon, was that they were all expensive.

"I went down to the crossroads…."

With the words of Robert Johnsons epic blues ringing in my ears I set course for St Jean de Losne crossroads of the canals.

A few days later we arrived at St Jean and steering off the river entered the narrow channel in the right bank that led into a purpose built port. It was filled to brimming with canal boats of all descriptions, from large working péniches down to the holiday launches of a rental business that lay hidden in one corner.

With some difficulty, I found space and rafted against another boat that was tied up at the visitors jetty of Blomfleurs Marina. Once lines were secured I set off for the marina office only to find that it appeared to be deserted. After pacing up and down for ten minutes, I noticed that the office staff were in an adjacent room where they were successfully ignoring any distractions, like customers. If they kept ignoring me much longer, I might have developed a inferiority complex and joined the Cistercian Friars. Instead, I poked my head into their inner sanctum, waved a €50 note and said I would like to give them money. Even then their reticence to budge did not inspire confidence, plainly this intrusive foreign person was intent on ruining a perfectly relaxed social meeting with possible work.

A large somewhat severe woman eventually detached herself from her desk and came to see what I wanted. Following the usual mixture of Franglais that passes for communication, it was agreed that the very busy patron could spare time to talk to me the next day and so a rendezvous was made to discuss the work in question.

At the appointed hour, Monsieur Blomfleur Jnr. arrived right on time but before even examining the boat, he opened the conversation by saying that in his opinion he did not think such a large job could be done. "C'est un grand travail monsieur."

We were later to discover that he really didn't want to be in the boating business at all, but strangely his dream was to be a delivery driver and he would have pursued that career were it not for his father's insistence that he inherit and run the family business. He had little interest or aptitude for boat repairs, whereas his sister who had both, was passed over for the male heir, but she had now left St Jean to work elsewhere. We also later discovered out that M. Blomfleur was afraid of his customers and would go to great lengths to avoid seeing them.

"Do you realize zis eez ze height of the season and everything in France closes down for *les vacances?* Do you also realize zis eez a very big job and will take a week, if it is possible at all and it will cost a lot of money?" He asked, raising upturned palms as if to emphasise his point.

"Yes", I replied nervously, and I proffered my open wallet and repeated the litany of boat owners everywhere: "Help yourself."

121

M. Blomfleur reluctantly agreed to give me an estimate, but explained that it was not possible to start doing it now, because everything must close for lunch. The midi is sacred in France, about the only thing you might find open before two o'clock in the afternoon is MacDonalds, but in the eyes of the French they are Philistines anyway and don't count, though this doesn't stop the Frogs consuming tonnes of plastic burgers.

That afternoon as promised, the patron returned to our boat with his chief *méchanicien*, Pascal, to prepare a quote and evaluate extent of the job.

Pascal was a cartoonist's dream, indefatigably Gallic, he was tall and lean with a moustache and goatee beard. He peered out at the world languidly from behind bushy black eyebrows and was seldom seen without a cigarette hanging from the corner of his mouth. Pascal spoke fluent French, as well as French and did I mention he also spoke French? When it was suggested that I would be his assistant to reduce cost and save time, I wondered how the heck I was going to translate technical terms such as: reverse gear linkage?

Pascal the grease monkey and his boss prodded the boat knowledgeably for an hour. They were like surgeons going through the diagnostic motions on a terminally ill patient. Eventually they looked at each other, shook their heads and without a word they departed.

I have since discovered that a lack of communication is a French norm, as it doesn't occur to them that you might like to know what is going on and whether the disease is terminal or not. When the dinner bell rings, they simply bugger off, with no further discourse necessary. At the time I thought this complete lack of dialogue was very strange behaviour, but now I realise they really just had nothing useful to say. Having collected the necessary measurements, they were actually disappearing for some quality thinking time over a few fags and a couple of litres of caffeine in the office.

Sure enough, later the same day M. Blomfleur returned, with a quotation that was expensive enough to cause a dip in the FTSE and had me running off to my computer to consult the currency exchange rate and find out how much this was in real money.

Following my successful resuscitation with a defibrillator and an intravenous infusion of Jimmy Buffett music, I accepted the deal and a contract was signed to carry out the addition. As the business was fully booked at present, it was suggested we go away and come back the following week , so that work could start on the Wednesday morning.

For six days we decided to enjoy a leisurely cruise further upriver. Rather than wait in St Jean de Losne. I decided to continue up the Petite Saône. This route allowed us the opportunity to swim in the slowly flowing river. Though the water was an evil shade of green, it was August and the temperatures were in the +30's every day so this was an attractive prospect.

Our first overnight stop was only 5 km away at a disused landing jetty in a sand quarry. There was very little shade, so next day we continued onwards to Auxonne about 12 km up river   where Napoleon Bonaparte as a 2nd Lieutenant in the La Fere regiment had two duty postings between 1788 to 1791 interrupted by a 6 months "holiday" in prison. The Artillery school and barracks he used are still operating to train soldiers, and the place has an air of living history. Boney would still be right at home there today.

Wednesday, one week later as agreed, we were back in St Jean de Losne excited and up early ready to start. By nine o'clock there was no sign of the *méchanicien* Pascal, so I went to enquire about the delay.

"Ee eez note 'ere ee eez zomewhere else!" Was the profound response from the office secretary.   Pascal had been called away to an emergency aboard a boat that had broken down upriver and was now a more urgent priority, so apparently the work could not possibly start until Friday!

We used our time to sand and varnish the woodwork in the rear bathroom as well as the wooden shower grates for each of our three bathrooms. To entertain ourselves we even stripped the varnish off the kitchen cupboards. To have any hope of resurrecting the timber work all the varnish had to come off and be stripped back to bare wood. This took most of the day and filled the boat with sawdust. The interior looked like a sawmill, it was 38 degrees in the shade and no shade. Not a good day.

Friday dawned, but again no *méchanicien*,

"Pascal   ee is zomewhere else. Zer is another emergency breakdown so It is not possible now to start until next Monday, but definitely Monday, I will set up ze cannon on ze jetty in case anyone calls with problems over le weekend." promised M. Blomfleur.

True to his word the following Monday and two weeks after our initial meeting he arrived first thing in the morning to announce "Today is the day. Please move your boat into the canal and through ze lock to the work area in ze canal and we start immediately."

Desperate not to miss our slot in the schedule, I dashed back to the boat, threw off the lines and sped to the lock at top speed, which is about the same as a gravid snail on Valium. We transited the lock at the entrance of the works harbour in record time, all thanks to the assistance of a very shapely lock keeper. Twenty minutes after starting up we were tied up to a long grey concrete work dock, poised and ready for the mechanic to begin.

No Pascal.

An hour passed and still there was nobody, so I went in search of the missing *méchanicien*. It took a while to find him, but I discovered him hiding from the rain that had blessedly started to fall relieving the summer heat, in the staff room. From behind a smoke screen of

Gaulois fumes that he was generating he promised me that he would arrive in ten minutes.

I have come to realise that the French use a different clock to the rest of humanity. Ten minutes can mean anything from twenty minutes to a couple of hours. Tomorrow, means sometime this week. Maybe. These are statements of intent, rather than a firm commitment to act at a precise time.

It bucketed down with rain that day, so all work on the quay came to a halt as workers sheltered from the deluge. There was only one bedraggled idiot to be seen still working outside. It was not Pascal, it was me. Determined that this job would be done no matter what, I had started working in the rain to demonstrate my commitment to the task, though I discovered later that the more sensible Pascal had been working on our steering console in his dry workshop. Unlike me, he was smart enough to come in out of the rain. At the time all I saw of him was his back as he climbed into his car to go home for lunch and he didn't return. Pascal had knocked off early for the day as a hydraulic line connector had to be ordered and come from Holland. More delay.

Trish had by now become part of the St Jean de Losne expat community. Monday was group walk day, Wednesday was book swap day. Friday it was off to the Laundromat for the weekly wash. Saturday there was a free Jazz band at the camp ground by the river.

To keep me entertained whilst Pascal toiled slowly, but thoroughly on our boat, the solenoid that should shut off the motor ceased to function. Pushing the dashboard stop button to shut off the engine was now as effective as throwing a marshmallow at a locomotive, the motor just kept right on running.

Off I went on my bicycle to buy a spare from the nearby charter boat base that had similar boats to ours, only to find that the Nanni diesel distributor for the whole of

125

France was closed for one month during August Holidays.

"Desolée mais c'est impossible!" Said the receptionist in the front office, as she explained politely that the entire European distribution for Nanni diesel part is based in France and rather than leave a skeleton crew to handle urgent orders, instead they close shop and shoot through for Summer holidays.   It seemed impossible to me that this could happen to an operation of this size. What a way to run a country? It was as if Ford had closed up shop for a month.

Fortunately, the charter boat mechanic took pity on me and rang around some of his mates, until he eventually found someone with a spare part in stock on the shelf. He arranged to have this sent to me and I was happy to reimburse him with a carton of cold beer. In France there is always a way forward, I was learning.

By Friday, Pascal had been working on the boat for five days and though it had taken a while to get him started, once the mood took him he worked well and was making an excellent job of our modifications. By three o'clock in the afternoon it looked like he might finish the job. Wrong! Without a word he suddenly disappeared in mid afternoon. It was the Assumption weekend and the village closed for a firework display on Saturday night. Apparently the village of Losne supported the monarchy during the French revolution and as such they do not celebrate Bastille Day on the fourteenth of July with the rest of the country. Just so the locals don't miss out on fireworks, a Pyrotechnic is held at Assumption instead, as the village's way of thumbing its Royalist nose at Paris. They celebrate what and when they want to. *Vive le Roi!* Luckily for them the guillotine is out of favour or they'd all be up for the close haircut treatment.

There would be no more work for three days.

Tuesday morning of week four dawned and Pascal was back on the job early. Standard parts wouldn't work, so

126

Pascal was having to custom fabricate some of the gear change mechanism. He appeared hourly trailing a plume of cigarette smoke, with strange pieces of plumbing, which he tried in, then muttered something in garlic and returned to his workshop. He looked like Dr. Frankenstein trying bits on his new creation only to find they didn't fit, then he would rummage through his junk pile of dead motors at the back of the workshop before emerging with another mechanical limb to try.

It was all too much for me. Whilst it has been unkindly suggested by some, that patience is not my *forté*, (All this time I had been holding it together pretty well for a control freak,) at this point I cracked and decided to do the electrical wiring myself to speed things up.

Two hours later I was finished installing the switching and alarm lights for the new console and still had time to check the gearbox oil and install the new stop motor which had finally arrived from the charter boat mechanic. Pascal approved my circuit diagram and wiring then retreated to his lair muttering about impatient bloody foreigners.

By late afternoon he was unable to get the new steering hydraulics to bleed properly. In spite of transfusing the master cylinder with enough hydraulic fluid to resuscitate Elvis, it stubbornly refused to animate and turn the rudder.

Surely work must finish today, completion seemed so near and yet so far away. In reality it was even further away than we realised, whilst installing components of the steering, Pascal had identified a completely different problem with the engine mounting bolts. There were only two left tentatively holding Brutus in place instead of the required four. Two bolts attaching the motor to the propeller shaft had also sheered off, if the remaining two broke we would be stranded with the Brutus rattling around loose, threatening to punch a hole in the bottom of the boat and sink us. Also the rear rudder mounting was flexing and threatening to come adrift. Failure of that would leave us adrift without steering, like the Flying Dutchman we would be fated to haunt the canals forever, unable to reach port. More delay, these matters had to be fixed.

Of course it was impossible to do more that day. We were so resigned to never leaving at this point, that we just shrugged off the new calamities.

A few days later Pascal refitted the drive shaft, while I repaired the steering mounting with a large piece of lumber that had conveniently fallen off a nearby fence and work ceased on the boat. Was it finished, surely someone would tell us? There was no sign of Pascal in his lair and the yard was uncharacteristically quiet, so I went in search of M. Blomfleur and sure enough he confirmed that the repairs were finally done. With true Burgundian charm he apologised for all the holdups and presented me with a bill that was considerably less than the one I had expected. We paid up, shook hands with the patron, thanked Pascal for his excellent work and within twenty minutes cast off before anything else could go wrong with the boat.

Standing proudly outside at our new helm as the newly varnished woodwork gleamed below, Trish and I felt like kids escaping school for the summer holidays. I was instantly delighted with the increased visibility and convenience afforded by the new steering position, it was also more companionable to sit side by side on deck under the cool shade of an umbrella. The movement of the boat generated a welcome breeze, as we motored away from the hot concrete wharf that had been our home for the past month.

The stress and mess of the long overhaul was behind us at last. Work that would have taken about four days in Australia, had taken five weeks to complete in France. It had been a sobering lesson in patience, but one that was not wasted on us as we realised that we must adjust to living in a different culture that works and plays by different rules. The French do not attach the

128

same adrenalin fuelled urgency to work as Aussies do, they work to live, rather than the converse, something many other countries including our own have forgotten in our headlong rush to pursue the goals of materialism.

Vive les differences.

Locked in, locked out, shorn and well fed

Lock keepers are a weird mob and of the many characters one meets travelling the waterways of France *les éclusiers*, as they are properly known, are certainly amongst the most entertaining.

Though not highly paid, to be appointed an *éclusier* to manage a lock is nevertheless considered a plum job. In most areas it appears not very demanding and comes with a low rent cottage next to the lock provided by the VNF (Voies Navigable de France). Many keepers strive to personalise these cottages and make them more interesting to passersby. This might mean a beautifully flowered garden with a collection of garden gnomes, or perhaps even a small café. Naturally some locations are more desirable than others, some are busier than others, but overall this is a cushy gig and much in demand. The regular lock keepers are a special group of people, and most do a great job.

Nowadays more locks are becoming automated, so eventually the job of *éclusier* will go the way of the typesetter and the travel agent, but in the meantime, these folk facilitate the passage through a lock by opening and closing the massive gates and operating the sluices that allow passage from one canal level to another. They also maintain the canal banks with the thankless task of endlessly mowing the wild grass that threatens to engulf the waterways and whose clippings give the water its characteristic green colour. In winter they dredge the canals and maintain the machinery that makes the system all work so well.

Many locks are relatively remote and those lock keepers are often eager to chat if given the chance. With only one exception, whom we shall meet soon, the *éclusiers* are a friendly mob and a great asset to the cruising experience.

In summer they have their annual holidays and are replaced by vacationing students. These young people have a wonderful time sunning themselves, while waiting for the next boat to turn up. Many install a lover in the lock house and it is not uncommon to have a red faced student emerge from the house pulling up his jeans, discreetly followed a few minutes later by a contented looking girlfriend, and why not? After all this is France.

Often students are quite entrepreneurial, such as the couple selling wine to the boats held captive in their chamber. Firstly the bloke would fill the lock with boats and then close the gates and deliberately very slowly operate the transfer sluices. Meanwhile the pretty girlfriend offered a selection of local wine to the boats and filled orders whilst the water transfer in the lock was occurring. Each bottle had a generous markup on the price, but still represented good value. They were so charming that I saw no one resist their sales pitch and wine was selling by the case load. By my estimate, they were probably making an extra €300 a day on top of their vacation pay and definitely adding interest, character and charm to the experience of passing through a lock.

On the Canal du Bourgogne, another imaginative lock keeper bakes delicious apple pies. Whilst the lock is filling he transfers a pie to your plate and your money to his pocket. Mmm…Delicious.

Others sell Farm eggs, Jams, marmalade and one *écluse* even had a mini theatre that featured local plays on Friday nights during the summer months.

Popular also are garden gnomes especially Snow White and the seven dwarves. Hundreds of garden

131

gnomes are often on display in and around the cottage gardens.

One enterprising keeper had covered the external walls of his cottage with antique farm and carpentry tools giving the place the surreal effect of a building that would not have looked out of place in Dante's inferno.

After the first hundred locks and just when you think you've seen it all, something different will come along to amaze you.

Some gates are operated personally by lock keepers, but on the smaller canals most of the locks of France are being automated. There is already a network of radar detectors, or self service contraptions that the sailor operates to control the machinery. Other mechanisms include a sort of garage door remote controller issued at the entry to a particular canal, as well as ropes to lift or twist that activate a lock sequence. These are very efficient and convenient, but have all the charm of a Coke bottle dispenser.

For now the *éclusier* remains one of the endearing characters of France but is under serious threat of extinction.

On major rivers locks can be enormous with depth changes of up to twenty two metres to accommodate working *péniches* of over two hundred metres in length. Sharing these locks with freighters that makes the Titanic look like a canoe, or can be a daunting experience.

In large commercial locks it is often desirable to contact the lock keeper on approach for instructions. On the Saône, Rhône, Rhine and other major rivers, lock keepers may want to put you in a queue until all the commercial boats have gone through. In addition, on rivers like the Saar, Rhine, or Moselle they often have two parallel pounds a large and a small one and may direct you into either size depending on prevailing busyness.

The keepers control all the traffic and are very efficient, if you can understand them, So instead of schmoozing up to the entrance of a lock and dawdling in as usual on small waterways, it is often necessary to talk to the *éclusier*, usually by radio. If you have ever tried to make a phone call in a foreign language and tried to understand the reply, then you will know how hard this can be.

 Below are the radio procedure notes I have written in our ships manual to minimise panic in these instances. Follow this protocol and either you should be okay, or at the least you will amuse the keeper.

How to talk to big commercial locks

What the lock-keeper really wants to know is:

Who are you?

Size is important, and anyone who denies it is handling themselves with tweezers. Are you a row boat or a mega barge? He really doesn't care about the boat name, so call yourself the Bismarck, or the Queen of Sheba if you feel like it, he doesn't really care, but he does want to find out what size vessel he has to accommodate.

Where are you?

Remember the lockie may have boats sitting outside his lock already and they all look the same to him. You might still be five kilometres upriver he can't tell on the radio. Be sure to tell him where you are at present. Commercial boats call up from a distance out and he will have their position tracked electronically on his monitor, small boats he has no handle on. I personally wait till I can see the whites of his eyes before I call the *éclusier* so that he knows where I am and I park out front where he can see me.

Are you heading upstream or downstream?

He needs to know which queue to put you in, does he fill or empty his lock to prepare it for your arrival.This is going to take time as the large locks are the equivalent of draining or filling 50 Olympic swimming pools

133

To get into a manned lock you have four choices:

Tailgate another boat and hope to get in: This is not popular, most commercial locks have a sign outside stating that it is mandatory to contact the keeper before entering. The green entry light you see, may be for a commercial boat approaching at speed from behind you.

Sometimes there is a waiting pontoon with a squawk box telephone: These can be unreliable sometimes, as it may not possible to get to the waiting jetty because of other traffic. Other times the box connects to a mobile phone so you may wind up talking to the irate and confused mother in law of a lock-keeper, who wants to discuss doubts concerning her son in laws parentage and why her daughter should never have got knocked up in the first place. Disturbing!

Mobile phone: An expensive option unless you have a local French phone card and assumes you have the right number for that particular lock. Often the information in cruising guides is out of date. Are you feeling lucky?.

VHF radio: We have a shiny new hand held yellow box for this purpose, forget the complex Euro speed dialing, Digital Selective Calling (DSC) system described in the text books, nobody appears to worry about it. After all who wants to announce themselves as "0234576291 calling?" When "Toul écluse bonjour, Saucy Sue ici ", is much more civilised.

Let's get started with a few examples of how to call up on the radio.
There is a lock coming. Find the call frequency either from the chart book or from signs on the shore. In Germany VHF becomes UKW, because K stands for

kurz which means short, so UKW is ultra short wave. By the laws of physics short wave is high frequency. I suppose UKW therefore ought to actually mean UHF, but it doesn't because the Germans like to be difficult, so look for signs on the bank like UKW 10.

In France just use the canal guide book to find the right channel and hope for the best.

Switch the radio on to the appropriate channel, turn up the volume then rotate the squelch control until it just cuts out the static. Listen in to make sure the air waves are clear, it's bad form to crash into another boat's conversation.

Prepare your schpiel. On the Rhine which forms the border between France and Germany, German is the lingua franca so try this:

"Schleuse (Lock Name), hier sportsboot Challenger One. Ich bin bei Schleuse. Ich möchte zu Tal (Downstream) or zu Berg (Upstream) Bitte."

The lock keeper will then throw big serves of Kraut at you, but he is mainly talking about his unhappy love life and how nobody understands him. Fear the wurst!

The key words you are listening for, are variants of *Kommen* (Come),*Warten* (Wait), *Gross* (Big lock), *Kleine* (Small lock), *Steuerbord* (Starboard), *Backbord* (Port)

Now you have to take a guess at what you think he really said and feed it back to him in such a way as to get a Yes/No answer that you will understand

"Sie haben gesagt, Kommen ins Kammer, richtig?" You said come into the lock right ?

"Sie haben gesagt, warten, richtig?" You said wait, right?

"Sie haben gesagt, die kleine(grosse) Kammer ? You said the little(big) lock, right ?

Sie haben ein kleine wille, richtig ?" You have a very small penis OK ?

Forget English, it isn't going to happen in most places. If you feel more confident faking French, then use that and you will probably be understood. The idea is the same but add a garlic and onion flavour to your mix. First move your hat to a more rakish angle and say the following in French:

Bonjour M'sieu, I know your love life is fabulous, because you are French and it is natural. I am Australian, not one of the despicable English who are not worthy to pick your nose, so if you are not too busy with your lunch, may I come into your lock please?

Loosely translated this would go:

"Bonjour Ecluse de Niderwiller. Ici bateau de plaisance Challenger One. Je voudrai aller en avalant (downstream) montant (upstream) vers Paris(Destination)."

The lock keeper now replies in a stream of fabulous language, that sounds like he is telling you he is hung like a donkey and his mistress should treat him better.

Listen for the words *Attendez* (wait) *Entrez* (Come in) *Merde!* (Shit, my wife has just found out about my mistress !)

Once again paraphrase your understanding back to confirm.

"Vous m'avez dit d'entrer l'écluse, n'est pas? " You said come in, right ?

"Vous m'avez dit d'attendre l'écluse n'est pas?" You said wait, right ?

We endured considerable pain figuring this all out and charges for confusing several lock-keepers are said to be outstanding in the EU court.

If all else fails, tail gate another boat into the lock as long as the entry light is green and you can see some room to tie up against a wall. If the lock gates don't slam in your face or eat your boat it will probably be all right. After all a number of our acquaintances swear by this rather risky method.

Unfortunately, getting eaten by closing lock gates can really happen and is a real possibility.

Once on the Canal du Centre I was cruising solo for a few days whilst Trish visited friends and was slowly exiting a lock behind another boat. I was taking my time, keen to make a clean exit in a seaman like fashion and not bounce off the side walls just halfway through the exit gate, when the automatic reset mechanism having detected that the first boat was safely out of the lock activated and the gates began to close. Unable to reverse or escape through forwards, it was one of those fateful moments when time seems frozen and you watch detachedly an event that seems to be happening to someone else. I was faced with the vivid vision of our plastic boat being neatly guillotined in two by the massive lock doors as they closed relentlessly towards me. My imminent doom had the moving effect of a ten megaton laxative. I leapt ashore and pulled the emergency stop cable, just as the gates engaged the sides of the boat like the jaws of a gargantuan shark. To my eternal relief the closing mechanism stopped immediately, but the boat remained in the clutches of the doors until an *éclusier* could respond to my emergency phone call.

Fifteen minutes later a bemused, but sympathetic lockie arrived to reactivate the stalled gates and release Challenger One back into the wild. Other than the blow to my mariners pride and a few scratches on the hull, all was well, but it was a lucky escape and suffice it to say that I no longer dawdle out of locks.

The ever efficient VNF also have a system for keeping tabs on which boats are making passage on a particular canal and where they are at a given time. Boats over twenty metres in length are fitted with

Automated Identification System (AIS) transponders trackers that identify them and their location at all times, but we small *plaisanciers* are a wild card in many ways not being obliged to carry such electronic wizardry. For this reason when traveling the waterways, I have found it important to make it easy for lock keepers to identify our boat by name when we arrive to make passage through a large commercial lock.

When we first took delivery of our boat from the charter firm in Castelnaudary, it came with the uninspiring moniker 'Challenger One.' Though this was not a total misnomer, as our sanity was indeed being challenged at times by new surroundings, lack of French and bits falling off the boat at regular intervals. It was nevertheless decided to rename the boat something a bit more French. We chose the name PARCE QUE which means "because" in French.

We started by removing the old Challenger One signage. However, with no name now painted on the stern we kept getting numerous requests at locks to identify the name of the boat. The conversation in French would run something like this. "What is the name of your boat *s'il vous plait?*"

'Parce Que.'

'Because what monsieur?'.

'The name of the boat is Parce que.'

'Because what?"

This exchange could go on for several minutes like an Abbott and Costello sketch, until eventually we would explain that it was "because we can", or like; "Why not?" and that this was a little joke in English. However it is plainly one which does not bear translation into French, still a little light would go on and the bemused official would stroll away muttering the equivalent of, "Idiot foreigners."

To solve this recognition problem, we designed a stern sign that declared the name of the boat PARCE QUE and listed our home port of Castelnaudary underneath

138

it. This would solve the identity crisis and mean that lock keepers at big locks no longer had to leave their ivory control towers, or lean precariously over the edge of the basin abyss to identify us but would be able to read the transom for themselves.

Trevor was heading back to Australia for a family gathering and agreed to get a name decal printed by a local sign writer, then bring it back with him on his return to France a few weeks later.

This he did and on the return journey he guarded the precious paper scroll with his life, so that it would arrive undamaged. All the way from Australia, he kept it on his lap, through three flights, across four continents, through the Paris Metro in rush hour and then finally on the long train trip from Paris, he nursed that sacred text.

When he arrived triumphantly at the boat, I took it from him with all the homage due the Dead Sea Scrolls and after a large amount of celebration wine was drunk and a few casual fireworks were tossed around the mooring to mark the event, we decided to put the sticker on our anonymous boat straight away.

I set about marking out lines on the boat to ensure we placed it straight and after an hour of adjusting the position of the lettering and a few more flagons of vino collapso to aid the calculations, we were ready for the grand unveiling. I stripped off the backing paper from the transfer with a flourish and presto, like magic, there was nothing there. Nothing, no name or lettering, nothing!

On closer inspection we found the stupid Australian sign writer had printed the letters in white, which laid onto a white hull just disappeared like money at a Boxing Day sale. Fortunately, the blow was cushioned by our prophylactic alcohol consumption and the situation was remedied a few days later when a local sign company printed the correct black letters PARCE

QUE, Castelnaudary, and the rebadging was completed.

Rarely one comes across an *éclusier* who has got out of bed the wrong side that day, or is just not a happy camper, but we had been warned that one of the lock keepers on the Canal de Bourgogne was just such a person.

We were enjoying a summers day cruise on the Bourgogne canal which runs through the very heartland of France when a number of boats heading the other way warned us to be ready for a less then pleasant encounter with a very rude and aggressive lock keeper. What none of them had mentioned was just which lock this dragon habituated, so for two days we entered each chamber nervously awaiting a confrontation.

The Burgundy canal has over 120 locks with often a lock every 1.5 kilometres, so by the time we did enter the dragons den we had forgotten all about the warnings. As we tied up our mooring ropes, a very large woman with dark hair pulled back in a bun and a face that only a mother could love, approached the boat and hailed me from the lock wall above

"Heh, Tête de noeud," came the gruff voice.

'Pardon?' said I, not understanding.

"'Tête de noeud!"

'Pardon?' Why was she saying "head of a nude" I puzzled, was this a new boating command?

'Tête de noeud!" yelled the woman re faced and with even more conviction.

"Desolée je ne comprends pas madame!" I responded confused.

"Tête de noeud.'Vous comprenez?" Her red face was now pulsing like a giant boil ready to explode

"Quoi?" What was this woman on about?

"Tête de noeud ! Tête de noeud ! Tête de noeud !"

This last outburst was accompanied by violent gesticulations apparently made to emphasise her point

140

and then suddenly understanding dawned on me. I remembered that a *Tête de noeud* is a scatterbrain.

"Ah! d'accord madame, vous m'insultez," you are insulting me, I replied with a happy smile of understanding that the mystery was solved.

This was all too much for the dragon, her head of steam was completely deflated and wasted on this uncomprehending foreigner, she stumbled off looking crushed, to operate the lock gates in silence. We exited through the gates of doom without another word from Madame. On reflection I felt a bit like Gandhi, even if my passive resistance had been based on a complete lack of understanding.

The other end of the friendliness scale would occur much later in the year on the river Yonne. It was early September and the young students hired to replace permanent lock keepers had all returned to their studies and the full time professionals were back on duty. After a run of unmanned automated locks it was nice to enter a manned lock and receive a friendly greeting from a real *éclusier*.

A short man of medium build, he was distinguished by a large round golden hoop earring in each ear and an engaging smile that revealed a large gap between his front teeth. After a short conversation about his recent family holiday in Toulon, he informed us that he controlled the next lock remotely by video camera and would be waiting for us to arrive. Never camera shy, we offered to dance for the camera at the next lock, then made our farewells and headed upriver.

Twenty minutes later we entered the basin of the next lock and true to our word whilst passing the monitoring camera we waved and danced a little jig on the roof of the boat hoping we had livened up his otherwise quiet day. We settled down and waited for the lock to start, but nothing happened. Then a few minutes later as the lock doors started to close, music began blaring out through the public address system. It was the

141

Australian national anthem, 'Advance Australia Fair.' Whilst we were motoring between locks the enterprising *éclusier* must have downloaded a copy of tune and it was now playing at a million decibels through the VNF loudspeakers. Not to be outdone, we fetched our outsize boxing Kangaroo flag on deck and joined in enthusiastically for the camera.

But the disco lockie wasn't finished with us yet, from the anthem he moved into AC/DC's 'Thunderstruck.' This we accompanied with improvised air guitar solos and head-banging that would have done the Bogan army proud. Still laughing as we passed the exit camera, we lined up on deck, saluted and sang the Marsellaise, the famous French surrendering song, after all one good turn deserves another.

Amongst the tasks on board there is always personal grooming. After a few weeks cruising through the Burgundy region, it was no real surprise when I woke up one morning, looked in the mirror and decided I needed a haircut. This might surprise some who know me well, as I am a somewhat follicularly challenged and don't have much hair left at all. There is a lunatic fringe running from ear to ear and a large solar collection panel on the top and that's as far as it goes. I think my style is best described as being "A wide parting." Nevertheless, I like to keep what little wool I have neat and so it was time to get a shearing. Trish has lovely dark thick lustrous tresses, so she needed a trim too, but as I had less to loose, it was decided I should pioneer the new experience of French coiffeurs and if I survived, she would consider trying one too.

Later that day as we were walking through a small rural village which shall remain nameless for reasons that will soon become apparent, I noticed a traditional barbers shop. The window display featured faded and curling pictures of mens hair products that were so old fashioned, that any day soon they might become new again as the wheel of fashion comes around again.

Though it wasn't possible to see inside, it was plainly a mens barber shop and the sign on the door said, 'Open,' so I decided to take the plunge and commit to the full country haircut experience.

I opened the door and stepped boldly inside to be immediately confronted by Madame la coiffeuse who was standing hands on hips inside the door to greet me. She was an ugly woman of indeterminate age dressed in slumped stockings, flat shoes and a grey coverall apron that might once have been white. Her grey hair was tightly drawn back in a bun giving her the severe appearance of a prison warder. Her disconcerting appearance was not my biggest problem, the smell in her shop was appalling. Piles of old newspapers were everywhere and the place reeked of cats.

Her shop was small and once I was over the threshold madame moved in behind me cutting off any retreat so that there was no way I could gracefully back out. Trish was still outside two steps behind me, she took one look and one whiff of the interior and beat a hurried exit down the street. The door slammed behind me, so there was nowhere to go but forwards. I took a seat on a decrepit looking bench next to another waiting customer and wondered how long I could hold my breath to avoid the awful pong. Madame returned to attacking her current clients tonsure.

as I gazed around the salon I noticed that beneath the tarnished and cracked wall mirrors, the work bench was littered with hair cutting tools. Hundreds of pairs of scissors, cut throat razors and combs all jumbled into quietly rusting piles. Cleanliness and organisation were obviously not priorities in this establishment and I could see no attempts at disinfection. I decided that was probably for the best as it might have upset the cockroaches who undoubtedly ruled the boutique at night. I sat there willing my olfactory system to shut down, but it was to no avail.

Eventually, Madame finished her ministrations and shook the hair off the coverall to join the luxuriant mat of cuttings on the floor and turned to welcome her next victim. I was still trying to figure out how to politely get out of there, when I realised that the man waiting next to me was indicating I should go first, so as not to keep my wife waiting outside in the street. I reluctantly climbed onto Madame's revolutionary (French revolution) chair and explained that I wanted a two millimetre crew cut. Normally that means out with the electric trimmer and the lunatic fringe is mowed in about two minutes flat, a simple request which leaves no room for error or misunderstanding.

There was to be none of that modern stuff for Madame, out came the hand clippers from under her pile of dodgy looking instruments and she went to work with a will. I could tell immediately that as well as cleaning, sharpening her tools was also not something she chose to waste time on. I am sure that they were sharp when she bought them, but as that was over a century ago, any cutting edge they once had was long gone. The pruning felt as if each individual hair was being ripped out by the roots. It took agonising ages.

After what seemed like a week, but was probably just the longest fifteen minutes of my life, Madame proudly handed me a mirror to contemplate the finished result. I could hardly see any difference, but happy to escape her clutches I smiled, nodded my appreciation, paid the bill and escaped to the glorious fresh air outside.

Trish reviewed my new style with its tufted freshly plucked look and laughed so hard she almost cried. Then she went to the *electroménager*, bought some electric clippers and did the job properly. After mt experience she tactfully decided that her haircut could wait a little longer.

Personal grooming aside, nothing is more important in France than food. The place is a veritable cornucopia of haute cuisine and there is so much to learn about the delicacies with which the French like to stuff themselves. Almost as interesting though is what food is not available. For instance, French cuisine hasn't really got it's brain around the whole vegetarian thing and the vegan persuasion is not expected or condoned in most eateries.

When we presented for dinner at an intimate Burgundian country restaurant a visiting vegetarian friend struggled to find a suitable choice on the menu. When our waiter approached she politely asked if there was a choice for a vegetarian. Somewhat perplexed by this unusual request, the waiter considered a reply and his face lit up as he proudly exclaimed. "But of course madam we ave ze lamb." I suppose that might count, it does eat grass after all.

Vegetarians should bring their own Mung beans and Alfalfa sprouts to France, because this country means business in the kitchen. If it flies, swims or crawls the French will shoot it and eat it, Frogs are an unapologetic nation of carnivores.

Watching French chefs at work is not for the faint hearted even amongst carnivores, particularly those that care about their cholesterol levels. Most dishes seem to start with a generous dollop of butter, add the ingredients, add a large amount of cream, then perhaps a little more butter to finish. Whilst the results are usually superb, it is a wonder that the entire population are not grossly obese, though it is true that the French diet has changed for the worse in the last ten years. Most restaurants now serve French fries with lunchtime dishes and portion sizes have increased to the point that makes finishing a four course *formule* meal, almost impossible.

In a shock to the national persona, recent statistics have also revealed that the French now drink less than half the wine they used to. Apparently, quality is now preferred to quantity. This is great news for those of us with cast iron palates, as the lesser vintages are available at give away prices in the supermarket. A good Beaujolais on the breakfast muesli is a total economic possibility for the devoted liver basher and cheaper than milk.

In provincial France the lack of international food variety is also very noticeable. The French feel that their food is the best in the world, so why would you eat anything else. Wonderful as French cuisine is, sometimes I hankered for some spicy food like Sesame Chicken or a good Rogan Josh. Searching the Asian section of a supermarket might land one a bottle of Curry Sauce and some rice, but usually that was about it. Chances of finding fresh Coriander, or Bok Choy, are as slim as a Parisian model. This meant that the discovery of an Indian restaurant in Lyon, or a Vietnamese in Auxerre became a special event when our chilli starved palates could receive a thorough scouring with a molten vindaloo, or a chilli squid noodle feast.

Still you've got to hand it to the French, their food really is the best overall. The Germans can't get past sausages and sauerkraut, the Italians will pizza and pasta you to death, whilst the Spanish just want to kill something (usually porcine,) cure it and put it in a bun.

Some of the greatest treats of French cooking are not the famous Michelin starred restaurants, but the working mens cafés. Hidden in nondescript buildings, they often have little in the way of signage, making them gold mines that are usually hard to find. Packed with a lunch time crowd of farmers and truck drivers they are usually in the strangest of out of the way locations. The locals know where they are and one can often find a three course set menu lunch with wine included for under eighteen Euros.

What is food without wine? There's probably nothing can beat sitting on the deck of the boat, ambling slowly down a leafy shaded canal on a summers day, with a chilled glass of Rosé in one hand. However understanding French wines and appreciating them is a treatise in its own right. Aptly titled in French, *Vins Francais pour les nulls* the big yellow book 'French wine for Dummies' became our booze bible. All my attempts to establish a wine cellar onboard were limited by lack of space and a tendency to drink the lovely stuff faster than I could buy it. I horrify my more knowledgeable shipmates by insisting on drinking the wine fresh. Forget vintage, why buy wine that has been lying around going off for years?

I admit that most of the time this was just stirring to get a reaction, but it rarely failed to elicit a long discourse from Trevor on winemaking, that would invariably involve the words 'Philistine' and 'peasant' and see him wander off shaking his head at my complete inability to appreciate good plonk.

Traditional French wine labelling focuses on the name of the vineyard, with no hint of the grape variety. Unless you happen to know that Alphonse du Berry makes Cabernet wines you are a bit torpedoed at the supermarket shelf when trying to choose the evening tipple. Our system was simple, we left wine choices to Trevor our wine buff. Anything over 10 € required team approval, at the other end of the scale, I was banned from buying plastic barrels of paint stripper for 4€ at the supermarket, which was probably just as well.

Food is not limited to the commercially available fodder in France there is also plenty of free 'bush tucker' if you know where to look for it.

One of my favourite dishes is duck. French duck is plump and juicy unlike the scrawny anorexic birds that pass for ducks in Australia. Sometimes though a duck fetish can get out of hand. I came on deck one morning to find the boat zig zagging erratically along the canal like a ball in a pinball machine. Trevor was at the helm and it wasn't until I got close and could hear him mumbling. "Here ducky, ducky," that I realised he was attempting his own duck hunt using a forty-six foot boat to run down his quarry. When his hunt failed to produce results, we consoled him with a visit to a local restaurant.

After that Trish drew the line at live bush tucker, if it needed skinning, plucking, or gutting it was not to be brought aboard. Naturally as a sensitive new age guy, I am too delicate to engage in such activities, but I must admit there have been plenty of opportunities when a couple of quick shotgun blasts out of the cabin window, would have scored us a very tasty meal.

Less homicidal forms of bush tucker, include olives in the South of France. De-stoned and soaked in freshwater to remove the bitter flavour, then spiced with garlic and rosemary these make a very welcome addition to the evening *apértif.*

Chestnuts and walnuts in season can always be collected along the canal paths, whereas in late summer, mushrooms and blackberries are plentiful as well. In particular the large variety of mushrooms to be found make this something of a thrill sport. Whilst 'Pick the magic mushroom', may be popular amongst the Russian roulette set, I have found that a safer solution is to take the collected fungi to the village pharmacy. French pharmacists are obliged by law to study Mycology, so rural pharmacies will happily identify the non lethal mushrooms, as a free customer service.

Not content to rely on the countryside for fresh food on morning I decided to start my own herb garden onboard. Off to the local bricolage on my bike I went and I soon had four empty window baskets fitted to the grab rails on the aft deck of the boat. Next stop was the village market where I bought a selection of herbs in pots. Arriving back at the boat proudly with my purchases, there was Trish waiting at the gangplank and knowing of my black thumb in the gardening department, she looked at the unfortunate greenery in my arms and said to the plants "Welcome to death row."

Fortunately for the plants, she took pity on them and oversaw their care and in no time we had become almost self sufficient in herbs.

But I have saved the most plentiful bush tucker for last. One of the most exciting things about early spring is that stinging nettles start to flourish. They grow in abundance by the canal paths everywhere in France and they are a wonderful food source that is completely overlooked by the locals. Nettles are among the most nutritious of wild foods. They make a delicious substitute for Spinach. When cooked, the sting disappears, leaving behind a delectable herb packed with more vitamins and minerals than a health food shop. It is truly a super-food and its healthful qualities are the ultimate bonus.

Try the easy, super-nutritious, and delicious soup described below.

SOUPE AUX ORTIES

Stinging nettle soup
Ingredients:
- 2 Tbsp. butter, divided
- 1 onion, chopped
- 1 tsp. salt, plus more to taste
- 1 lb. potatoes, peeled and chopped
- 6 cups chicken or vegetable broth
- 1/2 lb. stinging nettles Pick your nettles before they flower. They are best picked when they are 4-12 inches tall, before their stalks get too tough.
- 1/2 tsp. freshly ground black pepper
- 1/4 tsp. freshly grated nutmeg
- 1/2 cup heavy cream (optional)

149

• Sour cream, yogurt, or Horseradish Cream (optional)

Preparation:
1. In a large pot, melt 1 Tbsp. butter over medium-high heat. Add onion and 1 tsp. salt. Cook, stirring occasionally, until onions are soft, about 3 minutes.
2. Add potatoes and broth and bring to a boil. Reduce heat to maintain a steady simmer and cook 15 minutes.
3. Add nettles (I jam the pot FULL of nettles) and cook until very tender, about 10 minutes. Stir in remaining 1 Tbsp. butter, pepper, and nutmeg.
4. Puree soup with an immersion blender or in a blender or food processer in batches. For a silken, less fibrous texture, run mixture through a food mill or sieve.
5. Stir in cream, if using. Season to taste with additional salt and pepper, if you like.

Serve hot, garnished with sour cream or yogurt if you like.
Dust lightly with nutmeg and serve.

Makes 4 to 6 servings

My teeth are going yellow, so my dentist told me to wear a brown tie

Rodney Dangerfield

Trevor's brother Marshall is known to his friends as Diddley, after the great blues guitarist of that name, but bears no resemblance to him whatsoever. Diddley is a stocky farmer who is used to dealing with machinery and large wooly animals.. Like most Aussie farmers, out in the bush Diddley has often had to improvise to keep his farm machinery running far from the luxuries of a neighbourhood service station.

It was inevitable and sure enough one day Diddley came to visit and so it was little surprise that within an hour or two of boarding he took an interest in Parce Que's mechanical beastie Brutus below decks. The first thing he did, was to fix our throttle control, a repair that had been deemed impossible or at least prohibitively expensive by the French marine mechanics we had consulted.

"No worries mate, I reckon a couple of holes and a bit of fencing wire will do the trick" said Diddley. Half an hour later it was done. Next, he listened to Brutus and rapidly diagnosed that something else was wrong.

"That bloody thing vibrates more than my tractor, lets have a look at it mate." He said.

Down into the bowels of the engine bay he went and emerged sometime later smeared with several shades of oil and bilge water to announce. "I think your drive shaft has got a bit of a "woof" in it. If it was any worse, it would be mediocre mate."

I translated his rural rusticisms to mean, that the drive shaft looked bent and indeed it did seem to be wobbling as it rotated.

"Mate I'd get that looked at if I were you, before you come to a sudden stop right up shit creek without a flaming paddle" suggested Diddley.

Thus it came to pass, that I tentatively nursed the drive shaft as best I could and set an even slower than usual course for our winter refuge on the River Saône at Seurre where there was reputed to be a mechanic who would be able to address the motor drive issues over winter.

It was the end of September and the weather was cooling down for the long hard cold winter ahead. It was as if some heavenly power had pulled a lever to shut off summer as each morning became colder than the last. Plainly it would soon be too cold to stay much longer on our boat which was only designed for summer holiday makers. Parce Que's big glass windows so lovely with their panoramic views of golden corn fields in summer, now were frosted white in the mornings and radiated that cold straight into the boat. The boats diesel central heating and an electric fan heater were about as effective as a candle in an igloo and numbing cold lanced its icy fingers right through the boat in the evenings and at night.

Trish took to wearing a tracksuit to bed, then climbing into a sleeping bag which she next covered with two duvet covers and in the morning she still woke up feeling cold.

All along the route lock keepers were preparing to close up the some canals for winter, soon passage would be impossible as many of the smaller waterways freeze solid in the winter months. Even the large harbour at St Jean de Losne has been known to turn into an ice skating rink. Whilst it would be sad to put our voyage to Paris on hold, I set a course for Seurre and we travelled long distances slowly each day to make sure we were on time for the winter rendezvous without further mishap.

Enroute to Seurre on a crisp autumn day we motored through pastures and forests watching the farmers busy in their fields rolling up the last of the big cylinders of hay for winter forage. A smell of bovine fertiliser hung heavily in the air produced by the walking entrecôtes de boeuf that were chewing their cud contentedly in the verdant green pastures on either side of the canal. I was on the aft deck of the good ship with a glass of pastis and munching through a piece of crusty baguette, watching the sun as it began to fall toward the evening horizon to end a perfect day afloat, when all of a sudden it felt very draughty at the front of my mouth and I realised a tooth had fallen out. Well not exactly a tooth, but my one and only capped tooth had come unglued and was embedded in my snack.

What is it about teeth? They can be a pain when they arrive, a pain when they go and often a real nuisance in between. There's never a good time to have a dental problem. I once had a local barmaid as a patient in my dental surgery, who swore that the pork crackling they sold over the bar was responsible for breaking a tooth per day, so I guess it's not surprising that crusty French bread can be a bit lethal too.

Rural France is not known for its dental expertise, so my pulse shot up like a Sherpa going down Everest on a bike at the thought of looking like a local toothless hayseed for the next month until I reached Oz. I remembered seeing a billboard of supermodel Elle MacPherson, on which some wag had blacked out one of her front teeth and if she couldn't look good with a missing front fang, what hope was there for me? With bits of chopper in hand I pondered a possible solution.

My first thought was, out with the superglue, but I quickly discounted this, as the possibility of gumming up my mouth was a bit daunting and my dentist would have strong words to say when he had to remove the stuff to effect proper repairs later on. The only thing for it, would be to make some temporary dental cement. For this I would need a pharmacy to buy the ingredients, but we were in the middle of nowhere and it was nearly closing time.

As chance would have it, after consulting the chart I discovered that we were moored only about three kilometres away from the nearest village. Without further delay I unloaded a bike and pedalled off in the direction of salvation. A few minutes later I arrived in the tiny village of Héménaville, it felt like a ghost town, all the shutters on the windows were closed and if a tumbleweed had blown down the street it would not have been out of place. At the rear of a house I spotted a middle aged housewife getting into her car and approached her for help.

"Madame, pourriez vous me dit, s'il vous plait, est-ce-que il-y a une pharmacie dans cette ville?" I queried.

"Non M'sieu, the closest is in the next village which is ten kilometres away, in that direction", she answered gesturing towards the nearest hilltop.

Speed was now of the essence as closing time was fast approaching, could I get there in time ? About turn with the bike and off I pedalled at top speed. I hadn't gone far, when the canal path abruptly came to an abrupt end, so I took to the main road. Not only did it fail to follow the canal, but it rode the absolute crest of the valley ridge, up hill and down dale it went off into the distance.

The canals of France are bordered by towpaths, because in earlier times horses and child labour were utilised to pull the barges along and nowadays most of them have been converted to cycleways so one can usually follow a cycle path from village to village without traffic and without hills as all the waterways are flat. On a bike I don't do hills. I remain scarred after cycling four hundred bum crunching kilometres once in the Albany to Perth bikeathon. At the end of that week long event and once my saddle sore testicles came out of hiding, I swore that was it for cycling up lumpy stuff.

There was nothing for it, with the clock ticking and my remaining teeth gritted off I went on the road. In protest to the unaccustomed strain my bike immediately crapped itself and broke down. It must have seen the challenge of the hills ahead, and thought bugger this for a joke! My over enthusiastic changing gears had flipped the chain off and it had wedged itself between the wheel and the frame. Five minutes, much swearing and a pair of black greasy hands later, I was on my way again.

After a gruelling ride that would have won me a place in the Tour de France and had Bradley Wiggins shaving his sideburns and queuing up for my autograph, I arrived at the next hamlet and there, sure enough was a pharmacy.

Perspiring profusely despite the autumn cold, my hands covered in bike grease, I entered the store and queued up behind the diseased, the lepers, the hypochondriacs and other fellow sufferers, to see the person in charge.

I didn't have to wait long and explained to Madame Pharmacist, a tall stern looking lady, that I was an Australian dentist on holiday and that I had a problem with a tooth and needed some chemicals to make a glue. She looked skeptically at the short, red faced, gap toothed senior citizen with the dirty hands, dripping perspiration on her clean floor and with a sigh asked exactly what it was that I needed.

This was the next challenge. How to ask for Zinc oxide powder and Oil of Cloves in French? Fortunately, when

155

I wrote it down she instantly recognised the formula for Zinc Oxide, ZnO , and my trusty iPhone translated Oil of Cloves as *Huile de clou de Gonfleurs*,   which appeared to have meaning to Madam.

"How much do you want? she asked.

"Oh a couple of grams of powder and a couple of mills of *huile* should do Madame." said I and off she went into the back room to fetch it.

Five minutes passed, then ten and eventually some twenty minutes later Madame reappeared with a small brown bottle which had the sickly smell of clove oil that used to taint dental offices everywhere. She also presented me with a tiny handmade envelope containing two precisely weighed grams of zinc oxide. This was what had taken so her long, weighing the stuff out on a scientific set of scales with nano science precision. I didn't have the heart to tell her that I just ladled handfuls of the powder into a somewhat arbitrary mixture and then stirred till I had a putty like goo, which then could be slapped on liberally to the offending fang.

Successfully equipped with my supplies, I gingerly remounted the seat of pain for my return journey. By now the sun was setting and it was rapidly getting dark. The hills were no smaller on the return journey, but now there was no pressure of time, so I walked up the biggest ones. After half an hour, I realised that I was lost, had I gone past the turn off to the mooring spot in the dark? I decided to press on and five minutes later I was very relieved to spot the boat nestled behind some trees at the waters edge.

I staggered aboard to find an anxious Trish who had no idea in which direction to send the search party if I hadn't turned up soon.

I set to sterilising my tooth stump with two medicinal glasses of Rosé and another of Pastis just to be sure. Next I mixed up a paste of my precious glue, loaded up the cap and crammed in onto the tooth, *voila*, mischief managed, tooth gummed into place, vanity restored.

With my smile intact, it was time for the delicious duck dinner that Trish had prepared in my absence and we celebrated the end of another adventure.

Two days later we arrived at Seurre, where Alain the mechanic was tasked with examining the drive shaft and with winter ready to begin in earnest, it was time for us to head back to the sunny climes of Australia. I was sad to leave Parce Que after the adventures of the past six months and I felt mixed emotions as the taxi drove away from the marina. Though it would be great to see the offspring back in Australia, our voyage was only half complete. In spite of the many challenges encountered along the way we had not reached Paris, but at least we were our way.

A week after we arrived back in Perth we received an email with pictures that showed the offending drive shaft removed from the boat. It was a disturbing banana shape and ready to fracture mid way just as Diddley had predicted. The shaft, was apparently 'necking'.

Nothing to do with getting to first base at the prom, necking is an engineering term used to describe what happens when you bend a piece of metal back and forwards at the same point. The metal crystals become work hardened and brittle at the point of flexure and the metal constricts. This is the same as bending a wire coat hanger back and forwards until it fractures. In this instance the coat hanger was our drive shaft and close examination revealed that it was reduced to half its thickness at a point which had been hidden from our view by a worn bearing. Like a flexing coat hanger it could have broken at any time with catastrophic consequences. The drive shaft would have fallen out of the boat leaving us powerless in a river current and with the boat filling with water from the empty propellor shaft tube and sinking.

We were very grateful to have had the problems identified by Diddley before a failure occurred.

Well done farm boy.

Blanche and the multinational erection

Ships log: River Saône & Canal Rhône au Rhin

Year Two -May, June

After six months of enjoying the Australian sunshine, I was itching to get back to France and continue our voyage through the backwoods and villages that most tourists never get to see. Trish had decided that April was too cold for her in Europe and she had dispatched me solo to France.

This season I had promised her that their would be new boat rules, most importantly no more chaos. I had strict instructions that if I insisted on tearing the boat apart again, it had better be done before she arrived.

Secondly, this year's cruise was not to involve the acrid reek of fibreglass resin and the never ending repairs that had been an ongoing trial during our first season.

Thirdly, there was to be a progression of fine restaurants, some quality shopping and much leisurely sightseeing of historic ruins even older than me. This would be a season of immersion in French culture at the grassroots level and long unhurried lunches at charming bistros. Standards were to be raised meaning bargain price *formule* restaurants featuring French fries with everything were banned and if there was no tablecloth set, then such an establishment wasn't to be considered a restaurant.

Challenged but inspired by these strict new protocols, I set off for France three weeks ahead of Madame to get the DIY repair stuff out of my system and prepare the red carpet.

Garth, a great friend of mine volunteered to accompany me and provide free labour, as well as ensuring that adequate quantities of wine and beer were consumed at the worksite, thus ensuring proper lubrication of the workforce.

I first met Garth many years ago on a low budget ski trip to Austria. At that time he was an expatriate South African working in Europe with some dodgy Yarpie mates, to whom he was affectionately known as "the Hooligan." His extreme exploits on the snow, included a signature move in which he would stare over the lip of some sheer alpine precipice that was way beyond our beginners level and launch himself into space with his battle cry, "Death or Glory." This made him our natural leader and like Lemmings we would follow him over the most insane terrain.

The Hooligans' athletic après ski performances with such ladies as Ronnie Roommate, Helicopter and The Piglet was also the legendary stuff that one reads about in letters to Penthouse magazine. The sort of letters that begin 'Dear Penthouse, I read your stories each month and have always wondered if they are true, that is until the other day in Austria when…..' and end with 'I'd never let a daughter of mine do that'.

A consummate traveler, the Hooligan bounces from one place to the next with the indefatigable energy of a super ball and I hoped I would be able to keep up with him.

Our trip from Australia to France passed smoothly, apart from one rather embarrassing moment in Kuala Lumpur when Garth and I entered a hotel lift. Once inside we waited as the polished stainless steel doors doors closed silently behind us and stood there good-naturedly, charmed by the Malaysian elevator muzak, admiring the luxury of the wood panelling and were much impressed by the smoothness of the ascent. Indeed it was so smooth we didn't even feel the lift stop as it arrived at our floor. After a couple of minutes the doors had failed to open automatically and internal panic started to set in. As we waited patiently neither saying a word, I was contemplating how long Malaysian elevator rescue crews might take to arrive with the Jaws of Life and simultaneously experiencing the joy of a full bladder. Curse those beers at the airport, I knew the third one was a mistake. Five agonising minutes passed before we looked at each other and mutually arrived at the conclusion we that neither of us had actually remembered to press the GO button; the lift had not even started yet. Chalk up a seniors moment for the lads, we could have easily been stuck there for days.

Next morning our flying tube of death landed safely and taxied towards the terminal at Orly airport. It was unseasonably warm and sunny for April. A lack of rain had the locals complaining about a dry period *la sécheresse*, but in comparison to the dustbowl Australia we had just left the countryside looked beautifully green and lush to us as we drove a rental car southeast from Paris to Seurre.

After lunch in Seurre we crossed the River Saône and located the deserted boatyard of Monsieur Venoir. It was an uninspiring place in the zone technique area of town on the right bank of the river. There was a large gravel park with half a dozen boats of miscellaneous age and character propped up on the hardstanding, near a shed that looked like a recycled WW2 aircraft hangar, but there was no sign of M. Venoir or Parce Que.

Garth took off to search the nearby river bank where some commercial barges were tied up and soon found her, she was moored next to a rusty old barge and both boats were covered with a layer of pollution and grime. We discovered later that the dirt was a legacy of the Icelandic volcanic ash clouds over Europe that winter, but at the time it just looked like neglect.

Clambering over the barges we boarded Parce Que aboard and entered the cabin to find that the interior looked like a demolition site, all the floorboards were up and tools were strewn throughout the boat. *Oh merde*! There was still no sign of Monsieur Venoir, but as it was still midi and as naturally as night follows day France must stop, nothing is more sacred than lunch so this was not really unusual. At five minutes past midi M. Venoir arrived in his Citroën van, trailed by a large cloud of dust as he crossed the boatyard and pulled up in front of his workshop. He climbed out of his van and walked towards me moving with the rolling gait of the large centre forward of the French Rugby team he so closely resembled. He was huge, with massive shoulders, intermittent missing teeth, no neck and piercing dark eyes that peered out from under black hedgerow eyebrows. Not the sort of person I wanted to confront with 'Why is my boat not ready monsieur?' He was accompanied by a gangly youth who he introduced as Jean-Michel and thereafter referred to as *Jeune*. We all shook hands and returned to the boat.

Fortunately, my first impressions of both Monsieur and the state of the boat were deceptive, as he explained he had deliberately left the floorboards up and his tools aboard so he could show us all the work he had done over winter. Alain chatted amiably as he pointed out the intricacies of our new drive shaft and bearings, whilst *Jeune* replaced the floorboards and packed his tools away.

'*Merci monsieur Venoir, c'est magnifique,*' I said, impressed by the thoroughness of the repairs that had been required.

'*Avec plaisir Monsieur André*', replied M. Venoir as he presented his bill, which we paid immediately but I flinched as I visualised my account draining into his, simultaneously raising the GDP of France by several percentage points and restoring France's AAA credit rating.

162

With the boat squared away and our debts settled, it was time to cast off and find a berth for the night. Fortunately we didn't have far to go with a mooring available in town directly across the river and soon we were snugged up in the cabin opening the first vin rouge of the season.

The following morning I woke feeling full of the joys of the new season and keen to strike a blow that would enhance the comfort of our little floating gin palace.

"How about installing a washing machine?' I asked Garth. 'Last season we spent hours each week searching for a *laverie* to do our laundry and they're always dead boring and expensive, it's like feeding money to poker machines that never pay out."

"Why not mate? Let's get stuck in," replied the enthusiastic Hooligan.

To install a washing machine would be a quest, a sacred mission guaranteed to win Brownie points with the missus when she arrived in a months' time and as any bloke will tell you, you can never have too many Brownie points in credit. They are hard to gain and even harder to retain seemingly evaporating at the whim of one's better half. A washing machine would be just the thing to eliminate the drudgery of the washday pilgrimage and good for a windfall of bonus points and so it was decided.

Next morning after ingesting the mandatory *petit déjeuner* croissants and coffee from a nearby *boulangérie* and thus fortified with sugar and caffeine we headed south on the Saône towards a rendezvous with a white goods store.

It was a glorious day with unseasonal warm sunshine, that soon saw us clad only in shorts and T-shirts. The air was still and a gentle current was moving us in the right direction as we headed south downstream from Seurre. The new gold plated drive shaft and propeller loved their first outing and the motor was purring along instead of making the bone shaking row that used to

163

accompany us everywhere. In such perfect conditions it was little surprise that by mid afternoon we had arrived at our destination in the beautiful town of Chalon sur Saône and tied up at the welcome jetty. I stepped ashore and made my way up a small grassy rise to the port de plaisance office to announce our arrival to the harbourmaster and seek a berth for our visit.

'*Bonjour M'sieu* Brockis you are back again,' said the pretty young receptionist sitting behind a desk immediately raising my libido by five market points, only to have it crash like Wall Street as I realised it was her computer that remembered me and nothing more intimate. Nevertheless, even a digital recognition felt good, promoting a sense of belonging almost as if I had been down the street for just a few days instead of seven months on the other side of the world.

Once the mooring fee was payed and the boat repositioned to a berth on a guest pontoon, it was time to turn our minds to the mission in hand. It was Saturday and as the shops would be closed on Sunday and Monday, Garth and I decided to go straight to a nearby electrical store across the road from the port and get the show started without delay. The Hooligan doesn't wait around after all.

Before leaving Australia I had researched all kinds of washing machines from stone sinks and the village trough, to industrial machines capable of washing for the Queen Mary. Leaving nothing to chance I was a full bottle on the subject and I knew the brand and model I wanted, I had even checked that this store stocked it As an additional precaution I even Googled the shop from outer space. Turns out I needn't have bothered, DARTY was directly over a six lane motorway from from the marina, that was much busier than it had appeared on the satellite images. Close though it was if one was carrying a heavy washing machine even with the help of the Hooligan, I could see it was going to require more than a shopping trolley to get the machine back to the boat.

DARTY's is one of those big chain stores that sells pretty much everything. If you can plug it in they probably have it. Once inside the shop I looked around excitedly, but there were no washing machines to be seen. Damn! They had fridges, food processors, even electric toilets that could shred personal guano to microns, as well as plenty of other shiny toys that buzzed or beeped, but there were no washing machines.

"Il n'y a aucune machines à laver?" I interrogated the nearest clerk .

'Désolé,m'sieur, but all our washing machines have gone. We are renovating and they are in a tent outside.'

Apparently, I would have to buy a washing machine from Cirque du Soleil and stepping outside the store, there was indeed a large round circus tent occupying the car park, *Un Grand Chapiteau.*

Stepping inside through a curtained entry, I was disappointed not to be greeted by a man with a big red nose and clown shoes. Instead there was a pimply faced French youth sitting behind a computer looking very bored and out of place in his circus environment. I felt a certain sympathy for him, his boss could at least have provided him with a couple of lions, a whip and a chair to keep him entertained.

The perpetually energetic Hooligan shot off like an Exocet missile to locate our machine and disappeared behind a pile of cartons. I was too lazy to follow him, besides smugly I knew what I wanted and had colour printouts to three decimal places to prove it. It was me versus French retailing, what could go wrong? I confidently presented my printout to Monsieur le pimple and indicated the machine of choice. He studied the order carefully and then went to consult his own computer.

'*Oui M'sieu,* we do sell this machine, but we not have one 'ere, it will have to come from Lyon. But it could be here by next Monday, or if you wish it delivered, then Tuesday might be ze *possiblité,*'

'Parfait,' Delivery sounded good to me, it would avoid trying to drag the thing across a busy six lane highway and so before spotty and his garlic machine could change their minds I whipped out international plastique and the deal was done in a flurry of keystrokes.

We spent the intervening weekend scrubbing the volcanic debris off the decks and surgically preparing a receptor site into which we would graft the new heart of the bateau due to be implanted in two days time.

Monday came and was *passé.*

Tuesday dawned introduced by a rooster, its crack of dawn call penetrated the thin sides of the boat and propelled me out of bed more effectively than a prostate exam. I would have gladly strangled the bloody thing if I could have found it, but at least we were up and partially coherent. Would the washer arrive today and if it did, would it be the right one?

Mon Dieu! Mid morning a goods truck arrived at the marina.

'Did you want an old machine removed Monsieur? asked the driver as he climbed down from his cab.

'*Non merci monsieur,'* I replied. 'I am actually hoping to get a NEW one.'

'Then I have ze good news monsieur' he said and voila, two minutes later, a new washing machine sat on the dock in all its pristine enamelled glory. It was the right model, at the right time and in the right place. *Oh, Vive La France!*

Unfortunately, I soon discovered, it was even heavier than I had realised and hardly budged when Garth and I tried to move it. (We later were informed that there was a slab of concrete inside the cabinet intended to stabilise the spin of the dryer.) Not only was it unexpectedly heavy but it was also too big to go through the cabin door. Perhaps it might fit through the skylight roof if we could only get the damn thing across the gap between quay and boat deck, a space that loomed like the Grand Canyon and which threatened to take our new toy to the bottom if we slipped up during the transfer.

I stood staring at the machine for ages, as if I could move it across that great divide and onto the boat with willpower alone. It sat there like a monolithic menhir staring back as if mocking my puny attempts to shift it. The irresistible force had met the immovable object and nothing was going anywhere.

As we pondered this impasse, who should sashay by but two enormous gay Scottish bodybuilders.

"Any chance of a hand with lifting this machine gentlemen?" I enquired.

"Certainly Jimmy," replied the larger of the two, in a Glaswegian brogue you could have cut with a Claymore. "We'll just pop off to our boat for a wee minute and slip intae something appropriate."

As we waited for them to return, another inspiration hit me! The French had not yet been given the opportunity to make me happy and of course I must allow them the chance. With this positive thought in mind, I looked around and spotted a nearby crane normally used to launch small yachts on the weekend. I ran up to the port office and explained my problem to Madame.

'Quelle catastrophe madame!' (Why is the French word for catastrophe female?) "Is it possible to use the yard crane?"

"Mais certainement, monsieur pas de problème." She answered.

Within minutes, Jacques the port mechanic had arrived in oil stained overalls that seemed to have been made for someone twice his size and he had our new washing machine roped up and swinging precariously out over the boat. Though it was suspended from the

167

crane only by an unsubstantial looking piece of rope, it nevertheless descended safely through the boat skylight, as easy as kiss your hand and landed gently on the saloon floor.

We had just disconnected the crane, removed the telltale ropes and thanked Jacques who disappeared into his shed to avoid any further attacks of work, when the two gay Gordons returned dressed in black muscle singlets and camouflage trousers. Their bulging muscles were freshly oiled and looking very butch, they appeared powerful enough to move mountains let a lone a puny laundry device.

'Thanks lads but we managed without you,' said the Hooligan skillfully failing to mention our use of a crane.

'You wee men are right stronger than you look.' said the larger of the Scots coyly. We're proper impressed wi you boys" They were so impressed, that Hooligan and I had to start talking about our wives and making blatant heterosexual noises to get them to go away, so we could begin installing the new addition.

Connecting the washing machine still required many trips to the bricolage for plumbing bits, but the job for once was uneventful and Blanche as we named her, became our pride and joy. For the remainder of the season we would spend many happy hours in front of her screen, watching clothes tumble around and around inside, a bit like watching reality TV with bubbles.

There are so many different nationalities involved in boating that showing off your national identity is important to all boaters. Most bumper drivers bring along a national flag from home and display it on the back of their holiday rental. Some even have a collection of flags flying like colourful bunting as if to say, 'Take your pick and guess where we are from.'

For me flying the national flag is a cunning trick I use to entice aboard drinking buddies of a similar linguistic bent.

To this end I have tried several different flags on Parce Que because the Australian national flag is not well known overseas. With the Union Jack prominently displayed in the top left corner we were usually mistaken for a Pommie boat. To counteract this I took to flying a boxing kangaroo flag, the Aussie sporting banner. I thought this would definitely establish our identity, but after several polite enquiries as to why we had a flag with a big mouse in boxing gloves on it, I decided it was time for a rethink.

The boat was registered in France so the correct flag etiquette is to display the French Tricolor at the stern and any other courtesy pennants at the mast. This is fabulous in theory, but in practice was not so easy to do as we didn't have a mast or a flagpole. Various attempts to raise a makeshift spar with broom sticks, gaffer tape and cable ties had proved unsuccessful and had resulted in either the flag flying upside down indicating distress, or at half mast inferring a death aboard.

Frustrated by a lack of success to fly our ensign properly, I ordered a magnificent mahogany flagpole from a local eco boat supply store. A magnificent and shapely piece of highly varnished timber subsequently duly arrived with a note in French attached, that suggested that the production of this item had devastated several acres of Amazon rainforest and apparently I was now on several wanted lists as an eco vandal. Damn!

By now Trish and Garth's wife Jane had arrived and joined the boat and one day while this crew were off replenishing our dangerously low wine and duck supplies, I bravely decided that I would erect the newly acquired flagpole by myself.

The rain had just stopped and Parce Que was moored side on to the jetty in Chalon Sur Saône. A stiff breeze was blowing from the north pushing the boat hard against the pontoon jetty. As I studied the job, I realised that I wouldn't be able to reach the mounting site at the rear of the boat by leaning over the stern without immersing myself in the green water of the Saône. To improve access I decided to push the boat off the jetty and pull it around so that the stern would then be tied end on to the jetty. This should go fine as long as the breeze didn't catch the boat as I tried to manoeuvre, in which case it would take off and I would find myself wind propelled dragging behind it and heading toward the Mediterranean.

Just as I started to coerce the boat around with a rope tied to the bow, a little elderly grey haired English woman saw what I was doing and asked sweetly if I would like a hand. Now I am not proud, and replied,

"Yes please, latch on that rope Grandma and pull."

The two of us strained trying hard to haul the boat around against the breeze but with little success. This didn't go unnoticed by a bloke on the boat next door and after a few moments of enjoying our struggle, a Dutch skipper bizarrely attired in bathers, dressing gown and Persian carpet slippers jumped off his boat and clapped on the rope as well. With the efforts of all three of us, we soon had the boat secured with her derrière to the jetty.

I tried to clamp the flagpole fitting on the stern railing, surprise surprise, it didn't fit. The three of us stood scratching our heads wondering what to do next.

By now another neighbour, a German, had joined our group milling around studying the problem.

"I haff a massive pair of high tensile Krupps steel pliers zat vill be goot for zis," he proposed.

Two minutes later he returned with a large set of pliers and was successfully compressing the jaws of the mounting clamp onto the railing.

I inserted the retaining screw; Buggeration! The Allen key wouldn't fit the head of the retaining screw and there was no way to tighten it and secure the mounting bracket.

"No problem," said a Swiss gent who had been observing from the neutral territory of his yacht and he hurried over with a handful of tools.

At this point we had five people on the job. The English dowager and the Dutchman steadied the boat, the German squeezed the clamp shut, I held the boat fitting in place and the Swiss burger tightened the screw. Within minutes the fitting was mounted. We all shook hands and made comments about international détente, peace and harmony.

The boat was swung back to the jetty and tied up and the celebratory beers were popped to toast the new erection and everyone went there separate ways.

The heavily laden crew were most impressed on their return when I showed them the new erection and even more impressed with my tail of international cooperation.

At last I knew what flag to display from my mast, forget kangaroos and national pride, in future I would fly the European Union flag with its circle of stars signifying the cooperation of the EU countries, it seemed most appropriate.

A few days after the grand installation, the hottest start to summer for a hundred years arrived following the driest spring for fifty years. The locals were carrying on about it like a bunch of frogs on a hot tin roof.

"Oh la la, La secheresse c'est le fin du monde." they wailed.

Naturally to me everything still looked verdantly green compared with Australia, where drought means conditions as dry as a dead dingoes donger and I failed to see what they were whinging about. In truth, by local standards conditions really were a bit dire and at some stage unless there was some serious rain soon there

171

were going to be water shortages across the country which could mean low water levels and the closure of some waterways.

Over the next days as supplies threatened to dry up, even filling our drinking water tank became more difficult. Water supplies on boats are finite, so all guests normally get a welcome aboard briefing warning them to go easy on the shower duration and that washing hair, for those that still have it, is a stop start operation to conserve the aqua.

Knowing that everyone had been warned to be conservative with water, when one of our guests announced that the shower had stopped mid lather up I firstly thought that the water pump had packed it in. However, after much tinkering with the delivery system I discovered the real problem, our storage tank was as empty as Beau Gestes' water bottle. So we were in the middle of France miles from the nearest Cordon Bleu restaurant, with no water, in the middle of a drought.

All was not lost I unmoored and set sail for the next town of Clerval in which the guide book assured us there would be water supplies aplenty at the port de plaisance. Until we arrived there we would have to remain hydrated with wine. Problem?

To reach Clerval involved a beautiful cruise along the River Doubs passing through green forested valleys whose sides loomed high above us and were garnished liberally with ancient forts originally built to control the river trade. We were sailing on mirror sheen waters through some of the most beautiful yet seldom visited countryside in France.

During the Second World war the dense forests of this region were the territory of the French resistance, the Maquis, who led the occupying Germans a merry dance through its dense foliage. Many savage conflicts were fought here.

I was just imagining these running gun battles on shore, when an incredible bang came from inside the

172

cabin and we came to a sudden stop. It sounded like a muffled explosion or at best Brutus had fallen clean through the bottom of the boat. Trish bounded onto the upper deck as horrified as I was. A moment later we both simultaneously realised that the noise had been the boat hitting the rocky bottom. We had run out of water again and were aground.

The drought affected river level was so low that venturing out of the marked channel by a even few metres, which was normally not a problem on such a wide river, had resulted in disastrous consequences. Parce Que was aground and sitting like a shag on top of a large rock.

After putting life jackets on the best bottles of wine and assuring myself that the Pastis bottle was undamaged, I checked the hull and found that we did not appear to have sprung a leak, good news indeed. unlike One bloke we heard of in a similar situation and who had put a hole in the bottom of his boat effected a successful temporary repair by stuffing a Camembert cheese in the breach and taped it in place with Gaffer tape. No such advanced catering would be required today and with a loud scraping noise I reversed off the obstacle then made our way back to the main channel. A bit shaken by our encounter with terra firma we continued on towards the next oasis to try and refill the empty water tank.

By lunch time we were only one lock away from Clerval where according to our guidebook water should be available. As we entered the unmanned automatic lock just upstream of the village I noticed an warning to Mariners posted on the lock-keepers window. The bits of French I could fathom said something about running aground in Clerval, so I consulted the pilot guide to find that it listed a sandbank right next to our planned watering stop and it urged caution.

173

Ten minutes later we passed under Clerval's bridge and as we entered the town. There ahead just as the guide book said was our watery oasis the port de plaisance.

Many small French towns like this one are keen to attract tourist boats. The locals think that we add to the picturesque atmosphere and economy of the town, so the village council build small marinas or jetties to encourage boats to stay. This is a great thing and everyone wins, we get a convenient place to moor and look decorative and the local shopkeepers take our cash in fair exchange. The facilities provided vary from a tiny pontoon jetty suitable for a single boat, through to elaborate floating marinas with power, water and bathroom facilities all included.

Clerval had opted for a two boat floating pontoon jetty connected to shore by a *passerelle*, or gangplank. Recently constructed from excellent materials, this would normally have been a great asset. Unfortunately, to save money the council had built the pontoon right on the inside of a river bend next to a sandbank and as any boater will tell you, that is always going to be a shallow spot. Sure enough as we approached, I was not surprised to find that the pontoon was lying askew hard aground in muddy shallows surrounded by weed and garnished by a chorus of very loud vociferous frogs. There was no way a boat could approach the jetty, indeed the city fathers had been so cheap that I figured they must be the sort of people who would buy their kids Hide and Seek for Christmas.

If this location had been any better it would have been mediocre, but as it was, the river level had dropped so low that now a big red sign read *Halte Fermé*. The jetty was closed, it had run out of water. There might have been a water tap there on shore but it no longer mattered because there was no way to get close enough over those sandy shallows.

Sometimes life gives one little indicators and running out of water three times in one day seemed like a big

174

sharp pointy one of them. We were just not intended to have water today it would just have to wait. *C'est la vie.* The good news was that we had no shortage of wine, so as I slipped the cork out of the first bottle of the evening, I thought to myself that as hardy mariners sacrifices would have to be made. There's no law against brushing your teeth with Beaujolais, after all this is France.

You come of age quickly through shipwreck and disaster

Phillip Dunne

Ships log: River Rhine & Canal Marne au Rhin

Year Two- July, August

It seemed like a good idea to go to Switzerland by boat. I didn't even know it was possible until whilst browsing a guide book, I noticed that if we travelled upstream on the Rhine for a reasonably short distance it was possible to visit the land of cuckoo clocks and Heidi. I had never mentally connected Switzerland with waterways other than Lake Geneva and a few rippling mountain streams running off over priced ski slopes, yet there it was, a detour that would lead us to the city of Basel.

It turned out that the landlocked Swiss even have a Navy, well more of a merchant marine really, but even that in the middle of continental Europe seemed about as relevant as selling sand to Arabs. The idea that we could visit Switzerland by boat, seemed as bizarre to me as travelling to Hawaii by bicycle. Even if it wasn't strictly on the way to Paris it was an opportunity too good to pass up, so it was decided we would give it a try.

Of course nothing on our voyage is ever straightforwards, so many times I had set a course for one place and got distracted and wound up in a town miles away lured by the promise of free parking or a good restaurant. There had to be a catch and indeed there was. This time the catch was that we would have to motor Parce Que with her tiny antiquated engine upstream against one of the worlds most powerful rivers, The Rhine. Would we actually even be able to make ground motoring upstream? How strong was the current going to be?

Traveling east across France on the Canal Rhône au Rhin that links those two major river systems, the closer we got to the Rhine the more we heard tales of strong torrents that ran sweeping all before them. Everybody had a story of doom. One German told me the tale of a barge whose engine had failed and how it was swept away unable to manoeuvre, until it hit the arch of a bridge where the hull wrapped itself around the abutment, peeled open like a banana and sank with the loss of all hands.

Then there was the legend of the Loreley Rock. In early times it was said that there lived a pretty naked blonde woman, who distracted skippers from their work with songs and I suspect a spot of twerking, so that many an entranced captain ran his ship into the rock and was crushed by the swirling river. Feminists might argue that this served them right but even though I'm as ready as the next bloke for a bit of nubile eye candy, that sort of price struck me as a bit too high.

The real challenge was that Brutus is secretly powered by two geriatric Hamsters on a treadmill. On a good day they deliver the power of a small lawn mower and on a bad day all the magnificence of a Fiat Bambino with the handbrake on. This means we have no power to spare and navigating against a current rumoured to be faster flowing than our flat out top speed did not seem like a good idea.

Fortunately, just as I was at the point of giving up the idea and turning back I met Günter, a happy Swiss skipper who assured us that at this time of the year the Rhine here in the south was tamed by multiple locks that regulate the river to make hydroelectricity. Günter pointed out that one could check daily on the internet the prevailing current and that we should be able to go uphill safely to Basel. Probably!

As we completed our cruise through the beautiful valley of the Doubs and approached the junction of the canal and the Rhine itself we came upon two lock entrances to the river, one a beautifully designed flying wing structure sculpted in concrete and designed by the famous architect Corbusier in the sixties. This proved to be for commercial traffic and we were directed by radio towards a smaller entrance upstream that is operated for canal gypsies like us.

As we waited our turn to enter the lock chamber and descend to the river below we became aware that even in the shelter of the canal, uncharacteristically there was current swirling around us.

At last it was our turn to enter the lock and we descended to the lower level of the Rhine. The lock emptied and the huge gates opened in front of us and out we went into the stream heading upriver towards Basel. What a relief it was to find that the current was only flowing at about 3 kph which meant at our top speed of 7 kph we were still making ground over the bottom. Thus at walking speed we spent the rest of the day inching our way upriver until late that afternoon we reached the outskirts of Basel and found ourselves at the famous Tri-point where three countries meet. On the right bank Germany becomes Switzerland and on the left bank of the Rhine is France. So at one point on the surface of the river our ship was simultaneously in three countries at the same time. That seemed about the right time to call the customs post onshore directly opposite the Tri-point and ask for permission to enter Switzerland.

"*Guten Tag*, do you want us to land and show papers." I radioed to the frontier post.

"No problem, not necessary, welcome to Switzerland," was the immediate reply.

Several kilometres further upstream we pulled into the *Sportsboothafen* and tied up next to a long narrow wooden boat that stripped of its windows and paintwork looked naked. Onboard were three black bare chested Rastafarians who were sanding the woodwork prior to varnishing the entire boat, doubtless for a Swiss banker with deep pockets as it would be a mammoth job . Their dreadlocks were bouncing as the lads worked to the to the sound of a very large ghetto blaster blasting out Jamaican Reggae.

We tied up and a very large black dreadlocked face appeared at the cabin window and exposed a set of white teeth in a smile that flashed so brightly aided by a large gold tooth that it could have caused skin cancer.

"What be you frum mon?" said the teeth in fluent Bob Marley, which I interpreted as a greeting.

Not exactly the lederhosen and dirndl dressed welcome we had expected in Switzerland, a couple of Alpine horns and a cheese vendor would have been more appropriate, but at least these natives were friendly and generously helped us to moor our boat in a nearby berth before they returned to their own ship for a little ganja time.

I was about to step ashore when Rosy the harbourmaster turned up, she was completely disinterested in our attempts to pay for our stay and much more focussed on whether we had anything suitable to barbecue. Apparently, there was to be a harbour party on the jetty that night to celebrate Bastille Day and we were all invited. Basel was off to a good start.

That evening twenty of us from different countries and all speaking a plethora of tongues assembled on the quayside. As we sat on oil drums and planks under an awning of old boat covers and tarpaulins we looked like a scene more reminiscent of the finest shanty bar on a Caribbean island then a bankers yacht club in the heart of Switzerland. The wine flowed and as it disappeared

179

so did our shyness, we all seemed to understand each other more and more and before long were swapping stories in pidgin English, Norwegian, Dutch and German.

During the evening it started to rain and fireworks that had been scheduled on the far riverbank in neighbouring France to celebrate the Bastille day holiday were cancelled, but we were under shelter covered by a faded blue tarpaulin, the party was in full swing so nobody seemed to care.

After a shared BBQ feast assembled from the scrag ends of the galleys of ten different boats we went visiting each others vessels as sailors everywhere do. There were launches with inlaid walnut, granite bench tops and fittings that would have been at home in the palace of Versailles. There were converted barges built a century ago as well as sleek speedboats that looked fresh from running drugs into Miami.

The boat visiting included the pride of one Swiss skipper, whose taste in interior furnishing was a perfect replica of the Moonlight Bunny Ranch the famous brothel in Nevada. The cabins were upholstered in crushed purple velvet, with overhead mirrors all atmospherically lit by hundreds of tiny LED chaser bulbs. The jovial rotund owner and his petite wife proudly showed off their decor seemingly unaware of the implied heritage of their décor.

Basel itself was a joy to visit, with its cable ferries across the river, medieval centre which included the history of its city emblem the terrifying Basilisk, it beckoned us to stay longer but our timetable couldn't allow a longer sojourn if we were to reach Paris this year. Regrettably after a way too short visit of three days we rose early to make a start downstream towards Strasbourg.

Since our arrival the river had risen, it was now swollen by the heavy rainfall that had been falling continuously for the past few days and the current was flowing even more swiftly than before. Fortunately, this time we would be travelling with the stream. Our first challenge would be to extricate ourselves from the narrow box pen deep within the marina.

Before getting underway I studied the current that was flowing through the harbour and I could see that getting out would be a problem. We were moored in a box with our bow facing into the flow. To leave the pen, firstly we would have to drop backwards out of the box, then go sideways twenty metres until we reached the main harbour channel. Next reverse fifty metres back out of the narrow entrance channel to reach the open river.

I had never seen anyone reverse so far down a long channel before and certainly not in a fast current and I wasn't sure it was even possible to do it. There was no one around to ask for local knowledge, so I scouted around the harbour again and was relieved when I spied what appeared to be a sheltered turning area upstream but deeper in the marina. If I could only get out of the box pen and into the channel, then I could go forwards upstream into the turning area where the water looked calm enough to make a very quick about turn and shoot down the entrance channel with the stream behind me. It sounded like a good plan. But that was what Colonel Custer said at Little Big Horn and look how that turned out for him.

Trish expertly cast off our mooring ropes and I applied full power. Parce Que shuddered once at the unaccustomed open throttle, she dropped back out of the box then fought her way sideways into the channel against the current and then upstream she pushed until we reached the turning area which still appeared quite calm. So far so my plan was working, so I started to make what I hoped would be a very rapid about turn and that's where everything went badly wrong. *Merde!* I had misjudged the strength of the current below the calm surface and as soon as we were side on to the flow of the river the boat was picked up there was a sickening crunch and we smashed bodily side on against the boats moored in their boxes. We were stuck, harpooned on the bows of those boats like a shish-kebab, unable to move forwards or aft.

The current was too strong for us to pull the boat off with either the motor or ropes, so I was very relieved when the harbourmaster Rosy arrived. Rosy took one look at the situation, shrugged and said,

"This often happens here. Now we will need the rescue service and the Police"

Nice of them to warn us!

Next thing we knew the fire brigade had been summoned to rescue us. Within minutes the police were first on the spot and they proceeded to look authoritative and a bit menacing, as they began to cordon off the area with yellow crime scene tape.

The fire brigade arrived twenty minutes later in a large ship with red emergency lights flashing. The fire ship was 40 metres long and too large to enter the marina so the skipper moored outside and the crew proceeded to disgorge three high powered rigid inflatable dinghies into the river. It was turning into a big operation.

In a very professional Swiss manner, ropes were attached to a winch on the shore and to another large winch on the ship. It all took time to orchestrate but an hour later after much consultation and precision adjustment of the cables, on a signal from the coordinating rescue chief we were unceremoniously winched off the moored boats and back into the main channel. Now facing the correct way we escaped into the outer harbour, moored safely and then returned on foot to thank our salvers for their help, but not before the local media crew had showed up to immortalise the event on film. I am pleased to say we made front page of the Basel newspaper next day. The article was very polite and forgiving, the words idiot, incompetent and dopey were not used at all, though that was certainly how I felt.

Although there was some minor damage to the moored boats, which was to gladden the hearts of our insurers, Parce Que escaped unscathed save for a few scratches, the real damage was again to our pride. It seemed that the dreaded Rhine had exacted a toll from us after all.

Next morning as we headed north downstream the fast flowing current was behind us speeding passage towards Strasbourg, what a ride we had. Instead of our normal sedate 8 kph, Parce Que was surfing the flow at a record breaking 16 kph. Trees on the bank flashed by and we even overtook the occasional cyclist on the towpath, a feat never to be repeated. But the river wasn't finished with us yet. Even that joyride eventually had its price when we were unexpectedly struck by a large bow wave from a passing freighter and two of our bikes that had been inadequately secured on the bow of the boat broke free. One fell straight over the side the other slid back and forth on the front deck almost in slow motion as the boat rolled violently. I couldn't leave the helm to try and grab it and after several side to side oscillations with annoying slowness it pitched across the slanted deck and abandoned ship into the depths of the Rhine never to be seen again. There was no way I could stop in the fast flowing current and in the murky water there would have been no way to find or retrieve our steeds so we carried on towards Strasbourg. Score two for the river.

I hate cruise liners. Having a short attention span the thought of being shut up in a luxury prison is abhorrent to me. This in a circuitous fashion leads me to the tale of how I came to have a similar kind of expensive French experience with hot and cold running five star luxury. Firstly, a bit of my back story.

I was deported from England to the colonies at an early age, when my family emigrated. My father accepted a colonial position at the new fledgling medical school in

183

Perth, Australia and decided that the family was going too. My family travelled on the SS Iberia a P&O passenger ship and we were accommodated in first class, courtesy of the University of Western Australia. There were no other kids on the ship unless they were hidden in the cheap seats or the hold and after a three week journey from Blighty in 1957 we arrived on the flyblown docks of somewhere called "The Port of Fremantle".

The new medical school proved to be a bit of a challenge for dad as their one roller bandage and piece of string were in use when he arrived and it took time to get a real surgical department started. Over the years things improved and today I am reliably informed that the school even boasts a rusty penknife along with all its original equipment.

In a major tragedy my favourite Davy Crockett cap pistol was lost in the big move to Oz, (probably nicked by a stevedore in Bombay,) I was most upset and demanded without success that we return immediately to the UK and look for it.

Anyway, in some strange way the whole voyage and loss left me emotionally scarred on the subject of cruise ships. I hate them. Okay, so I realise things have changed somewhat since the Titanic stopped for ice cubes and that there are 20 – 30 somethings cruises operating out of Miami that make Sodom and Gomorrah look like a day off for slackers. Nevertheless, there are entirely too many big luxury steel slabs floating around the ocean. These are usually crammed with elderly dowagers, whose idea of a thrill is a morning lecture on Phoenician pottery followed by a nap, then lunch, another nap, afternoon bridge and then a session of strip bingo before dinner. So when I explain that I accidentally trapped myself in a similar environment perhaps you will understand my abject horror.

You have read about my "Torture the Tourist" hobby, the enjoyable game in which I pose as a Frenchman and amuse myself by sending American tourists in the wrong direction. (At time of writing, I have a tour party of beauticians from Idaho hopelessly lost in the sewers of Paris.) Though this game can be hours of fun it does carry a modicum of risk, that one day one of my marks will speak better French than I do, in which case exposed, I will have to *allez-y, trés vite* out of harm's way.

Thus with the selfish intention of self-preservation in such an instance in mind, I decided to give myself a linguistic safety margin by improving my spoken French. Bearing in mind my short attention span, conventional tapes and self study were unlikely to work, what I needed was an escape proof intensive course, living, breathing and excreting French, 24 hours a day. As there was no cruise ship offering such a thing I went for the next best option, and booked a week in a residential language school.

I found what looked to be a suitable place near Bergerac in the Dordogne and booked in. Trish as usual had more sense, she suggested that the whole thing sounded like a French version of St. Trinians and she decided to go walking in Britain instead.

On arrival in Bergerac, I was met at the train station by a very attractive French lady who introduced herself as Madame Stephanie. This was a name that I instantly connected with suspender belts, fishnet stockings and a French maid giving remedial homework. Perhaps this was going to be fun after all? The only other student waiting at the station was a twenty something blonde from the UK, who seemed nervous but friendly and confessed she was a beginner at speaking French.

After a short drive in an elderly Peugeot, that from the smell appeared to run on a mixture of onions and garlic, with an ignition system that involved a combination of cursing and twisting wires together

185

under the dashboard, we arrived at the Château. It was a beautiful traditional three storey building in the French Louis XIV style, set in a lush garden at the end of a long manicured driveway, and right in the heart of the verdant green Dordogne countryside. A large swimming pool with an adjacent tennis court completed the image of an exclusive luxury resort.

Everything about the accommodation was top quality, old school sophistication. Unfortunately, so were the remainder of my fellow students. Four elderly dowagers and a couple of senior citizens with their wives could be seen wobbling round the grounds on Zimmer frames. (They had to be wives, no one takes a mistress that geriatric on a slap up all expenses paid holiday like this.)

The school was run by an expatriate Pom, called June. I think she had probably moved to France when UK schools no longer had a demand for rah rah Hockey sticks matronly Margaret Rutherford types. Perhaps Trish had got the St Trinians thing right after all?

Next to arrive was *le professeur*. He was a short man, somehow very French, he was wearing a dirty soup stained pink shirt under a beige jacket whose crumpled appearance suggested like its owner that they had both seen better days.

The next morning we started our schedule. The day began with an excellent breakfast at 8 am. Of course by then I had been up for ages, read War and Peace, had a swim and kicked Junes dog for good measure. It took the crumblies another hour just to find their false teeth and attach the relevant prosthetic bits, so there was a bit of delay getting going each day.

Breakfast was followed by classroom lessons, all entirely in French. In fairness, *Monsieur le Professeur's* teaching expertise far eclipsed his lack of personal hygiene and his bombastic orations on the glory of France and things Frog were excellent. He did try to gloss over the French Army's need to fly the white flag so frequently and he did also try to convince us that the Maginot Line was a magnificent tactical success instead of the unmitigated disaster that almost bankrupted the country. His argument was that it had tricked the gullible German Army into avoiding it completely and invading France from the North instead. Cunning sausage eaters! Then again we all have a few strange ideas at times so he was entitled to his.

Following morning coffee, the group changed classrooms for a lesson with Madame Stephanie. This was much more disciplined. Madame Stephanie's room had lots of props. Not in the good way I had hoped for, there was nothing in black latex or rubber. During her sessions, though I tried hard, I couldn't even get a remedial spanking. Instead she had lots of charts, word games and notes with which she demonstrated her consummate teaching skills and even gave after class homework.

Afternoons involved a visit to a centre of local culture. Prof Alexander was in his element with old stuff. Cathedrals had every element of their construction dissected and described at escargot pace, with dear old Alex showing great reverence for the Holy Catholic Church that had erected them. Needless to say the poor peasants who lived in mud huts nearby eating *cochon merde*, and actually did the graft to build these marvels of religious glorification didn't feature at all in his *histoires*.

To escape all this culture, I tried to hide in a confessional booth, only to discover it was occupied and open for business. The priest asked me how long it was since my last confession and didn't seem pleased when I told him that if he wanted to confess me he was going to need a large baguette, bottle of vino and the rest of the week.

So there I was, trapped in a five star hell and after three days of intensive Cordon Bleu cooking, intra-venous vats of wine and non-stop French, I had lost the will to

187

live but any hope of escape was impossible. Even if I tunnelled out Great Escape style the nearest village was miles away.

Just when it seemed that things couldn't get any worse, they did. One evening after dinner I was forced to watch an incredibly tedious French documentary about spotty French primary children in a rural village school condemned to learn eloquent French. Quite why the school bothered escapes me, as the little ankle-biters were perfectly happy at home on the farm shovelling cow pats with their parents.

According to the documentary, the poor little sods were dumped in an *école maternelle* at the age of four, where in between sobbing pathetically for their mothers, they were forced at gunpoint to learn to read and write. The whole school thing was a bit militaristic and the documentary tirelessly teased out every nuance in the life of French four year olds for an entire school year. It felt like ten years in a gulag to me. Poor little buggers.

At the end of the DVD, Madame Stephanie (about whom I had long since stopped fantasising), made the mistake of asking the class if they liked the film and looked enthusiastically at me for a reply, hoping to spark a conversation. She seemed a bit put out, when I said that I would rather have a vigorous colonic irrigation with hot Jalapeno peppers, than be forced to watch that sort of thing again. Naturally the dowagers thought it was wonderfully sensitive and that it had great artistic merit, but what would they know? After all they even liked opera, which is well known to be the sound of dying cats scored to music, a cacophony that would even make Beethoven Roll Over and have Tchaikovsky singing the blues. (Well said Chuck Berry!) There was no escape, so there was nothing for it but to batten the hatches and see it through to the end of the week.

After seven days of indoctrination, I am pleased to report that all my tribulations were not in vain. I can now fluently tell a French waiter that the food he has served me isn't fit for my intestines and that his wine is not good enough to scrub my toilet with, (but that I will drink it anyway) and I can do it in several new and interesting ways. All of this done with a smile and a *savoir faire*, that would leave a Parisian waiter weak-kneed, humbled and seriously considering a career change.

I also now understand why at a domestic dinner, the fork is set on the table with the points down and how this is essential to world peace.   *Oh la la, quelle difference!*

Riveting stuff, but has it made me a better would-be Frenchman?   Strangely enough I think it has.   This backdoor entrance into the convoluted mind of the French helped me to understand such Gallic riddles as; how did a stunted dwarf like Nicholas Sarkozy ever get to marry Carla Bruni and why one must avoid a terminal faux pas such as serving wine before the main course is placed?

I shall probably never be the same again, my transformation means that now I'm afraid of language courses, as well as boring cruise ships both full of the living dead on their last bingo filled hurrahs.

By August after our individual excursions, Trish and I were safely back aboard the boat. We passed through the beautiful city of Strasbourg and were making our way west along the Canal Marne au Rhin which connects the river Marne to the Rhine.

One sunny afternoon we were cruising along a particularly narrow section of canal whilst enjoying the dulcet tones of Madame Sarkozy on the radio and all was peaceful in our little aquatic dwelling. This was canal cruising at its best, no currents, schedules or stress.

"Look out bumper boat ahead" cried Trish.

Sure enough there was a large rental boat approaching us in an very erratic fashion. They had just left a rental base which we knew to be located only a kilometre or two upstream ahead of us and now were in the process of zig zagging from side to side down the canal towards us. They appeared to have little control, as their boat bumped into the left bank, ricocheted off the right bank and then back again, apparently unable to steer a straight line. As they advanced towards us and the gap between our boats diminished, I was at pains as to see how I could avoid a head on collision. What had started as a joke now looked like an imminent expensive nautical pile up. I slowed up but still they came onwards at speed, bouncing from bank to bank and monopolising the whole canal. Meanwhile, a boat which had been traveling behind us was rapidly gaining ground and coming closer and closer toward our stern. As it approached within earshot, the unmistakable sounds of an operatic soprano drifted towards me. Behold, there on the front deck was a larger than life buxom Broomhilda who was giving her larynx an operatic workout that would have done a foghorn proud. I hate sopranos, they make strangled cats sound good and there we were, sandwiched between a Wagnerian earbashing and a kamikaze bumper boat. The whole thing was surreal and being unable to either go backwards or forwards, my options were limited. Collision was moments away and it was inevitable.

I was just about to assume the brace position, when at the last second out of nowhere there appeared a *sablière*. These are large holes dug in the sides of canal banks to quarry building sand, a resulting scar is often left there to fill with water and become a mini harbour. A quick turn to starboard saw me safely out of harms way into the safety of the narrow *sablière*. No such luck for the unwitting tailgating Broomhilda whose climactic oratorio turned fortissimo as she let out a blood curdling scream as the oncoming bumper impacted with her boat. The bumper pilot and his missus burst into tears and Broomhilda was pitched into the drink, whereupon the young couple compounded her problems by poking her with a boat hook in a ham fisted effort to rescue her. Meanwhile, I pulled neatly out of the safe haven behind them and continued merrily on my way as if nothing had happened, ignoring the debacle in our wake. After all Madame le president was in fine voice that day and it would have been wrong to interrupt her.

A few days later and a hundred and fifty kilometres further east it was half past September and the weather had started to turn cold. We moored in Lagarde, a tiny Lorraine village in the middle of nowhere but boasting both a marina and an excellent restaurant named PK 209 in which we subsequently enjoyed many excellent meals.

Parce Que was put to bed in a box pen, cocooned for winter and the crew departed for home and warmer climes. We had reached the latitude of Paris but for now our second season was over and the city of lights would have to wait until next year.

The Great Champagne Scam

As the time approached to return to the boat in France for our third season, I received news by electronic carrier pigeon that two Australian boats had sunk at their moorings. The story spread like wildfire through the boating community and about as welcome as a fart in a space suit. There were no specific details such as whose boats they were, or even why had they sunk, just the cold hard facts that two privateers were now sitting on the murky bottom, creating a habitat for marine wildlife. All owners feared the worst, that their pride and joy was sunk and turning into a creature of the Black Lagoon and I was no exception.

I hadn't received any news concerning either the wellbeing or demise of Parce Que, but this didn't mean much because the French are not renowned for being proactive with their communications. Parce Que could easily be sitting on the bottom of the canal for over a month before anyone had a brainstorm and decided it might be a good idea to tell the owner about it. In France everything is slow-tracked by escargot mail. For reasons that continue to baffle anthropologists email for business has yet to become popular amazingly they continue to rely on faxes. It's not that the French don't have computers, I think it is more that if they can't shake your hand, or put quill to parchment then a digital message is seen as impersonal and only for the lesser races like the English. Thus in the event of a disaster the first I would be likely to hear about it would be a politely phrased letter along the lines of:

" Bonjour Monsieur, how are you. The weather is very pleasant this time of year, isn't it? I hope your family are well and enjoying the beautiful sunshine in Australia. By the way a little matter; your boat does not appear to wish to float and has been resting underwater for a month, do you think there is a problem perhaps?"

Interestingly, though surface mail from Europe can still take a month to arrive in Oz, a French invoice will however show up with the speed of Concorde.

For peace of mind and with a healthy dose of fearing the worst I contacted Peter, an Australian friend living nearby Lagarde. Pete was was able to reassure me that Parce Que was still on the right side of the surface and not pretending to be a submarine. He was also able to furnish me with the full story of what had happened to the affected boats that were both moored in Montceau les Mines, a port on the Canal au Centre to the south of Lagarde and famous for the huge ugly cooling tower of a nuclear reactor that overshadows the town.

It transpired that an Australian and a New Zealand owner with boats both moored in Montceau les Mines had received emails from a friend living aboard a barge nearby, informing them that their boats had sunk at the jetty where they were tied up for winter. An initial attempt by the harbourmaster to raise the boats by pumping out the water had begun too late and it had failed, so the boats were underwater. To make matters worse French bureaucrats were discouraging any further salvage attempts by threatening big fines if any resultant pollution leaked from the wrecks. *"Mon Dieu,* Imagine le paperwork?"

Imagine also the difficulty of trying to mount an international rescue mission from Queensland to France, but that is exactly what one of the owners decided to attempt. Armed with some large inflatable float bags and a big sack of optimism, he took the next available plane bound for France. Twenty four hours later on arrival at Aéroport Charles de Gaulle, his jet lagged eyes propped open with toothpicks, he hired a car, stuffed it full of his rubber inflatables and headed south.

On arrival at Montceau les Mines the situation he discovered both boats were underwater sitting on the shallow muddy bottom of the canal but both were still attached by their sterns to the jetty.

His first job was to clear the cabin of floating debris. This meant swimming in freezing cold toxic green canal water, but with all orifices plugged in he went. His commitment was admirable it was a miserable job but it had to be done if there was to be any chance of refloating the boat.

Once the interior was cleared of flotsam, two air bags were placed in the front cabin and a locally rented compressor was attached to inflate them and displace the water. The huge grey bags distended and slowly filled looking like a couple of pregnant elephants had squeezed inside the cabin and were now trying to burst out through the windows.

At first, it looked like the boat might move, but by the time the bags were fully inflated, it became obvious that there was not enough lift and the boat failed to budge from the bottom. A third air bag the size of a baby elephant was inserted inside the front hatch and pumped up, but this also failed to raise the boat.

By now the local bureaucrats had arrived on the scene and were threatening even more intimidating penalties for any pollution emanating from the boat. When all their rescue attempts had failed and with the threat of such big fines hanging over the uninsured vessels, the owners decided to cut their losses and reluctantly abandon ship. A local company equipped with mobile cranes, was persuaded to accept both boats gratis and our man returned disconsolately to Australia.

The story didn't end there, because 3 weeks later the French salver had pulled the boats out of the water and when he examined them he found that the cause of the sinking in both cases was fractured water intake valves. Before leaving in autumn, as a precaution the owners had replaced older style brass screw gate inlet valves, in the boats hulls, with new stainless steel lever action ball valves. During the winter, water had frozen inside the ball chamber of the valves and its expansion had shattered the stainless steel outer casings. It had been a particularly cold winter, so that when the ice on the canal thawed during spring, in poured the water through the broken valves and down went the boats.

After hearing this story you can imagine how nervous I was about the welfare of our boat, as we had about six of these valves on Parce Que and we had been moored in the even colder north of France. Fortunately, I had been warned of this type of problem and I had trapped antifreeze in each of our valve chambers as a preventive measure. But would it be enough?

In May when Trish and I arrived at Lagarde in a rental car, we were heavily laden with boat spares and provisions ready to prepare for the season ahead. As we pulled into the marina yard, our worst fears appeared confirmed, there was no sign of Parce Que on the pontoon jetty where we had left her the previous year. Instead there was a dead cat floating in the canal in the spot and of our boat there was no sign. A polite but nervous inquiry in the port office informed me that Jacques, the *Capitaine du port,* had recently moved her to the far end of the harbour and sure enough covered in the dirt and the debris of winter, there she was disheveled, but afloat.

I stepped aboard and opened the first Champagne bottle of the season, it was great to be aboard our little floating home once more.

After cleaning up and reprovisioning, we headed west from Lagarde and a week later arrived in the most famous wine producing region in the world, the Champagne.

May is springtime in France, I could tell because occasionally it stopped raining. While the rest of France was bathed in glorious sunshine, grey clouds remained suspended over the Champagne region as if anchored to the famous flinty chalk hill slopes that produce the world's most expensive wine, but we didn't care, it was fabulous to be cruising again.

Some days later, we pulled into Châlons en Champagne and found ourselves moored next to a couple of career hippies from Queensland, Gary and Emily had been living on boats for years and Gary supported their lifestyle by consulting as a marine electronics engineer. Amongst his clients were the Swiss Merchant Navy, whose home port is land locked Basel in Switzerland the scene of last years shipwreck.

A ham radio enthusiast, Gary's must be the only boat still sending and receiving Morse code. Being tied up next door to him, listening to the incoming dots and dashes as he hammered his Morse key long into the night, was like a flashback to World War Two. I imagined an Enigma decoder rattling away below decks and half expected that at any moment the Gestapo would arrive for drinks and a friendly jack booted chat.

I was intrigued to find out more about this interesting couple, they appeared to be the sort of amazing people who are hidden within society if and great to discover if only one is lucky enough to spot them, so I invited them aboard for cocktails.

Sixty plus years young, the victim of a heart that had required complex nerve surgery, Gary's ticker now ran like a Swiss clock, but he didn't take a moment of life for granted. From sunrise to sunset he was on the go, stripping paint, installing some new labour saving device, or cycling for miles along the canal path, he just never stopped.

196

As the dynamic duo stepped aboard, I had just finished reading about the nautical cocktail of the season in *Fluvial*, a French boating magazine, it was a type of Kir, a popular summer drink seen in cafes and bars throughout France. It's normally a mix of Crème de Cassis a blackberry liqueur and topped up with white wine. The more upmarket version is Kir Royale which is Crème de Cassis topped up with Champagne. The boating magazine had gone one better than the Royale and substituted liqueur Curaçao for the Cassis which produces a magnificently fluorescent blue fizzy cocktail named *Fluvial Royale*.

What more appropriate drink could I proffer to these two interesting people when they came aboard? The Fluvials were a big success and one fluorescent blue potion led to another, as the tales of our individual travels flowed across the table as freely as the alcohol. After we ran out of Curaçao and champagne we cleansed with a couple of bottles of vino. At some point in the night, Gary told me that I was talking fluent Swahili and it was time to break up the party.

Late the next morning I woke up with only the sketchiest memory of the previous night and no idea of how I got to bed. I opened the saloon door, stepped out into bright sunshine on the deck and there was Gary already busily doing some morning boat maintenance.

"Morning mate how are you feeling?"

"Apart from a convenient bout of amnesia, strangely reasonable thank you" I replied." And you?"

"Bloody terrible, don't ever make those blue death cocktails again. I'd rather have a prostate exam from a four fingered leper, than drink that rocket fuel."

After a breakfast of aspirin and Alka Seltzer the world looked much brighter for all concerned and we cast off and made our way to the heart of the Champagne region, Epernay.

197

We tied up at the charming little port of the *Societe Nautique d'Epernay*, which is a quaint mooring on the river bank of the Marne, just outside the centre of town. Overhung by weeping willow trees that add a certain privacy and intimacy to the place. The port is normally something of a quiet backwater, but today the whole town was buzzing as this was the day that the 6th Stage of the Tour de France was due to start at midday. Welcomed by the harbourmaster with a glass of Kir Royale and handed free tickets to a champagne tasting at the house of Castellane, one of the most famous champagne producers, we felt right at home as soon as we stepped ashore. The centre of town was packed, as the locals were enjoying a public holiday to celebrate the national cycling extravaganza passing through their town. In true *Champenoise* style the golden bubbly was flowing freely and was being given away in the tourist office and in the streets, what a great place.

Suitably reinforced, we managed to find a barrier side spot close to the starting gate and on a curve in the road. There were three hours before kick-off and we set ourselves to wait keen to hold such a great vantage point. As it turned out we didn't have to wait long, the build up acts had already started with street performers who walked the route and charmed the crowds with sleight of hand magic tricks, as well as comedians and free samples from the event sponsors. This was followed by a parade of publicity vehicles all exotically decorated in a theme to connect the sponsors with the event. A giant cyclist wearing the famous yellow jersey, *le maillot jaune* of the leading competitor followed a giant Mickey Mouse from EuroDisney, massive motorised bottles of mineral water sprayed the crowds as free samples were thrown to the waiting faithful.

By now at the start line crowds were ten deep and the atmosphere was electric with excitement. Finally the riders took their places in the marshalling area one hundred metres behind the start line, then at the last moment the race leaders in the Yellow jersey, Red spotted jersey for the mountain climber and the White of the youth leader, royally made their way from the rear of the cyclists to take up pole positions of honour at the front of the peloton.

The pack advanced to the start line and then they were off in a high speed swirl of coloured lycra. The crowd roared *Allez Allez* and within seconds the competitors disappeared at high speed from view on their 205km ride to Metz.

Once the crowd began to dissolve I found myself standing outside the impressive Champagne house of Moët et Chandon and with Fluvial Royale now banned I decided that I had better investigate more about champagne while we were in the region.

Vintage, non Vintage, Prestige Cuvée, Grand Cru, Blanc de blanc, Blanc de noirs, Brut, Extra Brut, Demi Sec what did it all mean? I have a simple system when buying plonk, anything costing more than €4 is overspending and anything less is possibly life threatening or drain cleaner. Thus being somewhat of an ignoramus where wine is concerned, I set out on a liver sacrificing course of research to make sense of Champagnes. Someone had to do it after all.

Ça depend, literally 'that depends,' is a popular French escape clause for avoiding a definitive answer to any question. For instance ask a Frenchman how can the word for a bike, *la bicyclette* be feminine but *le velo* which also means bike, be masculine? Is it a girl or a boy bike?

"Ah monsieur, *ça depend*", It depends, will come the reply. Surely that is the perfect Catch 22, an answer without answering at all. I shall now explain how this is vital to evaluating Champagnes.

The first problem I faced in my research was that there are more than one hundred Champagne houses and 19,000 smaller *vignerons*, (vine-growing producers) in

199

the Champagne region, producing 30 million bottles of the stuff every year.

The second challenge was, "Just when is Champagne really Champagne?" According to EU law only wine made in the French region of Champagne can be legally called Champers. Many other countries may call their sparkling wines Champagne, but if the French are to be believed these are usually inferior low priced products, and not fit to wash your gumboots with. I learned that anything selling for less than €15, without the words "Champagne" and "Product of France" is not the real stuff.

When the French authorities decided that no other region could use the term *Methode Champenoise* to describe production of their wines, they magnanimously granted other regions the right to use the term *Crémant* as a compromise. Today *Crémant* wines are all made by the Champagne process in vineyards outside the region. But how do they stack up against the major league champagne brands?

A large part of the mystique and justification for the expense of Champagne supposedly comes from the amount of handling required to produce a good result. After the initial fermentation bottles are slowly turned by hand over a period of time, a process known as riddling, to coerce the sediment of fermentation to the neck of the bottle, were it can be removed in a freezing process after which the bottles are topped up with stock wine and varying amounts of sugar and left to ferment a second time.

This was originally very labour intensive and kept large numbers of the original Benedictine monks in a job for life. Nowadays, only a couple of houses still use the expensive oak barrels and hand turning in display areas, to wow the tourists, whereas in reality all the riddling is done by an automated machine kept out of public view, known as a Geopallet. The expulsion of the sediment is also now fully automated. The traditionalists say this showpiece facade of hand production justifies the high price of their booze. Interestingly, wine houses in the adjacent regions that use exactly the same Geopallet technology are able to retail their sparkling wine at €6 per bottle which rather shoots holes in this cost argument.

Today the Champagne of each house is a blend of grapes mixed by a master blender to replicate the style for which the house is known. So if these masters of champagne are merely blokes who can mix a brew of wines together to make the same style and taste every time, does that make the manufacturers of Coca Cola, another drink famous for its consistent taste and bubbles when purchased anywhere in the world, Master-poppers? Frankly, I reckon that the whole Champagne thing is a monster scam and a marketing exercise that has been successfully perpetuated for hundreds of years. Rather like DeBeers and the price of diamonds.

Next time you open a bottle of expensive fizzy grape juice such as a bottle of Premier Cru Vintage Champagne ask yourself, is it really worth twelve times the price of a bottle of *Crémant?*

Try asking a Frenchman that question and I bet the answer will be, ça depend.

I live in fear of a breakdown on Parce Que, not personally, but of Brutus going up in a puff of expensive smoke leaving us stranded on a fast flowing river miles from the nearest mechanic and decent patisserie.

As we were sailing along on a wide stretch of river one morning aided by a following current and making good speed, or God speed, depending on your belief system, we rounded a bend to discover a launch washed up in the bushes at the side of the river, the owners were frantically waving for help.

We pulled over to offer assistance and discovered that their motor had died. One minute it was happy next minute it was stone dead and without a pulse. The river current had driven them into the trees lining the shore where they remained hanging like a Christmas ornament, unable to get ashore because of the dense river bank foliage. They were mighty relieved to see help arrive after hours marooned.

We passed a line and towed them to the next village and left them to the fate of locating a mechanic willing to make house calls. In our experience they should have applied for residency in that village because they were going to be there awhile.

To avoid such misadventures I try to coddle our motor. Nothing is too good for Brutus. I chant incantations and by way of sacrifice to encourage the good spirits I change his oil twice as often as required and feed him only the freshest fuel from diesel stations on the southern slopes of grand cru oil fields.

With this coddling in mind, arriving late in the day in Largny sur Marne, I decided it would be a good idea to do a therapeutic oil change and boarded my trusty bike to the nearest supermarket for supplies. Big French supermarkets stock engine oil as well as Corn Flakes, which always seems a bit incongruous to me. After a long ride I had struck out at three smaller stores that actually only sold food. Undeterred, I asked for directions to the next nearest service station and was informed that it was only five kilometres away and so off I pedalled.

By the time I arrived, a "Business Closed" sign was just going up and a demolition crew of trucks and bulldozers was moving in. I could see the oil I needed still sitting in the shop, but the bulldozer pushed over the building anyway without even bothering to clear the shelves inside. I turned away disappointed and started for home empty handed.

As I crossed the bridge over the River Marne there on the far bank was another service station and this one appeared to be open. The bastards must have seen me coming and smelt my desperation, because they were demanding twice the normal price for their lubricant. and delighted though I might have been to Tigerise Brutus with an ESSO tiger in my tank, I decided not to enrich the coffers of Standard Oil. Luckily, as I left the station there was a sign for the largest supermarket chain whose store was said to be only five minutes away in nearby Chelles. Well, I assumed that was nearby, as I didn't have a map and the road signs indicated direction only. Off I went again.

I had travelled about six kilometres, when a hoarding by the roadside informed me that it was only another six kilometres to Chelles. Tactfully it neglected to mention that those few kilometres were all uphill. Having come this far I decided to press on and was eventually rewarded with both the supermarket and the oil I needed.

Heading for home and dutifully following all signs towards Largny sur Marne, I realised too late that I had made the mistake of my life, missed the correct turn and was now on the entrance ramp for a major motorway. Next thing I knew I was trapped in a concrete traffic channel with four lanes of traffic doing 130kph and me in the emergency stopping lane pedalling like a madman. There was no escape, on one the side of the road was a high concrete crash barrier, on the other side a deep ditch that I couldn't hope to cross even if I scaled the wall. Motorists angrily tooted the idiot on a bike and I pedalled like my life depended on it, because it did. It's amazing how motivating the horn of a loaded semitrailer can be when blown up ones backside from only inches away.

Eventually, I spotted an exit ramp and managed to return to suburban traffic. Still shaking like a dildo in a bowl of Aspic from the ordeal, I decided I needed refuelling and stopped in to visit Ronald McDonald. He wasn't home, but after swallowing a plastic burger and fries and a enjoying a romp in his playground, much to the annoyance of a couple of little kids, I felt restored and ready to continue my journey. I went outside into the car park but as I reached my bike I knew there was something wrong, I had lost my bike lock keys. Pocket search negative, restaurant search negative, bike lock search negative, Ronald's counter staff negative. Surely I hadn't thrown them in the bin when I cleared my tray? Head first into Ronalds bin I went, tunnelling past half eaten big Macs, slushies and wrapping paper until right at the bottom of the bin, there they were. Peeling off bits of burger from my face and removing the odd chip from my ear I set off for home.

The oil change was a simple matter after that, though I did manage to spill rather a lot of the old black oil into the bilge making it look like the La Brea tar pits, but by this time I was past caring, after all I had sacrificed mightily for that motor, so perhaps the Gods of Diesels would look on me with favour and a little sympathy and keep it running? Sure enough next day good old Brutus did indeed fire up and we cruised on towards our next port.

It was a week or so later that I awoke one morning with a hangover and a furry tongue which was stuck to the roof of my mouth like shag pile carpet glued to the ceiling and the thought occurred to me "Bugger, I may be an alcoholic! " This led me to wonder what the qualifications of a true card carrying boozer are, so I logged on to the internet to find out.

The American Medical Association defines Alcoholism as being characterised by:

A prolonged period of frequent, heavy alcohol use.
The inability to control drinking once it has begun.
Physical dependence manifested by withdrawal symptoms when the individual stops using alcohol.

Tolerance, or the need to use more alcohol to achieve the same effects.
A variety of social and/or legal problems arising from alcohol use.

Three out of four didn't seem too bad and fortunately they didn't mention a tendency to chronically sing Jimmy Buffett tunes, talk Swahili or collapse comatose on the bunk. So not having all the symptoms maybe this was a false alarm. Further research on the topic rendered the more succinct Unofficial French Plaisanciers dictionary definition.

"He or she who wakes up with a cleansing aperitif beer, keeps drinking until closing time and is never seen without a glass of wine in hand could possibly have a problem...... *ça depend!*"
I don't know why I should have worried really, after all someone wise once told me "If you are not on drugs and consuming big amounts of booze once you reach 60. What are you waiting for?"
Alex the bloke who told me that, looked about 90, so it was a bit of a shock when I learned that he was an early retiree of a meagre 53 years and that he intended to keep living his blurry dream as long as his renal function held up.   Alex used to be a chemical processing engineer and told me that he was still in the profession, only now he processes wine into urine for a job.
A typical day for Alex starts with a couple of wake up beers after breakfast, before steadying himself for lunch with bottomless pitchers of rosé that flow through the afternoon, before leading to a decent bottle of red with dinner. All of this goes to explain his patriotic eyes, blue with red whites and a red nose lit by a million exploding capillaries that would give Rudolph a run for his money on Santa's Christmas sleigh.

France is the world's largest wine maker and produces between 50 and 60 million hectolitres of wine per year, or 7–8 billion bottles, that's enough to fill 2400 Olympic swimming pools. Why anybody other than a statistician would want to fill a swimming pool with perfectly good booze is a good question. Living in a country where a half decent bottle of wine costs €3 and is available on every street corner, in supermarkets, groceries and petrol stations, it's little surprise that the temptation to tipple is always present. In spite of this the local culture is slowly changing and French annual wine consumption has dropped by three billion bottles to just four billion - the equivalent of one bottle per adult each week.

The French are alarmingly genteel for the most part about alcohol. A French mademoiselle would not dream of getting blind drunk, unlike her British and Australian Chav cousins whose weekend mission in life seems to be how to turn into a binge drinking slapper in the shortest time possible. The French are sippers, thus one glass of wine is served with the main course of dinner and that's it, no topping up.

Don't get me wrong, the country still has its problems with alcohol. In an effort to lower the road toll all French drivers must now carry an alcohol self-test kit in their cars. Whether this is to evaluate whether they have the minimum alcohol in their systems necessary to drive like maniacs, or need to go back to the bar and top up first, seems to be a mute point in the quest for motoring safety.

Pulling their weight courageously for the statistics around the larger towns there are also town drunks. These guys seem to favour hanging around ports, which until you get used to them is a bit challenging. Unlike English yobbos who hang around canals and pelt boats with stones and bottles for no apparent reason, these guys are invariably friendly and as you arrive will wave their half empty bottles in salute and invite one over for a drink. It is essential to moor upwind of them as they usually have a nearby bush for the team *pissoir* and will keep celebrating late into the night before disappearing to their cardboard châteaux under a nearby bridge.

Periodically the gendarmerie has a clean up campaign but a few days later they will be back, fundamentally harmless and exhibiting great Darwinism as they progressively eliminate themselves from the food chain they are usually harmless.

After studying a couple of these blokes and sharing a few stories with them, I decided I didn't yet fit their description of an alcoholic, but I was still a long way to Paris so anything could happen.

FLUVIAL ROYALE
Ingredients

> 1 bottle of Demi Sec Champagne or Demi Sec Crémant
> 1 bottle of Blue Curaçao
> Strawberries or Maraschino cherries for garnish
> Chilled Champagne flutes

Directions

> 1.   Add 1 measure of Blue Curacao to each glass.
> 2.   Fill with champagne.
> 3.   Garnish with strawberries or Maraschino cherries.

ENJOY

Paris is always a good idea

Audrey Hepburn

Ships log: River Marne to the River Seine

Year Three - August

Since setting out from Castelnaudary three years ago, we had braved many perils. We had been shipwrecked, boarded by pirates, and accosted by savage wildlife. Granted that we didn't have to contend with mountainous seas, dragging anchors, or the joys of seasickness that open water sailors seem to find so compelling and that the pirates were five years olds on the way to a birthday party, but in reality inland cruising is mainly a cushy gig.

Gourmet restaurants on hand everywhere in France, will beat the tinned stews that are customarily served up as haute cuisine on passage making yachts every time. Nevertheless, gutter crawling had nominally proven to be a risky existence at times. While the pirates were only five years old, the shipwreck was a real drama, as were the tales of the drowning pigeon and the floating stiff, that are about to follow.

I was enjoying my customary lunchtime glass of local chateau de cardboard, when I heard a splashing noise between the boat and the pontoon jetty. My first thought was that the fornicating fish were at it again, but when I investigated I found it was a pigeon that had fallen in the water and was now doing a very good impression of drowning. The high concrete banks of the canal meant it was unable to get out of the water and the bedraggled bird was making a very poor attempt at the backstroke. Because it appeared to be in some distress

208

and not enjoying its reincarnation as a duck, I fished it out and discovered that its leg was banded with a neat copper tube. Was this a carrier pigeon arriving somewhat late for the Great War?

The poor thing was all flapped out and the absence of bullet holes made me think it was more likely to be the weariness of old age that had caused it to crash land in the canal. The bird lay on the deck breathing but otherwise immobile and stared at me with two small beady black eyes that I found penetrating and quite disconcerting. Perhaps you don't find a pigeon scary, but I am still emotionally scarred from the night that chickens were turned loose in my college room back in my student days.

I returned late one night after a committed drinking session at the pub, to find several psychotic chooks had been released into my garret room and they were excitedly flapping and screeching and had turned the place into a farmyard. My first thought as one particularly athletic fowl clung to my lampshade, was that the vodka chasers might have been a bridge too far and perhaps this was a form of the D.T.'s. Just then the ringleader of the flock, a nasty vulture like creature launched itself at me and pecked my leg. Could the DT's draw blood? I stepped back outside my room and closed the door, but when I reopened it a minute later they were still there.

Having no idea how to wrangle poultry I had to go and find one of the other students, a hearty farm girl to remove them, which she did whilst muttering things like "Wimp" and "City boy." This experience left me profoundly wary of feathered critters, I'll eat them but that's as close as the relationship gets.

So now here was another avian creature viciously menacing me on my own quarterdeck and I was at a loss of what to do about it. Perhaps it would stay for dinner? It occurred to me that there were certainly a few delicious recipes for roast pigeon in our French

209

recipe books, but they would all involve a capital crime followed by some messy gutting and plucking. None of which I was up for.

We sat there staring at each other the pigeon and I, it was a High Noon standoff, we were both so equally terrified of each other that we were unable to move. The afternoon sun shone down on the vulture and after half an hour we both stopped shivering and it seemed to be regaining some strength. Fearful it was gathering itself for an attack I proffered a few bread crumbs from a respectful distance but it ignored my peace offering and without any warning and much to my relief it flapped its wings and flew away. The wildlife crisis was over.

A week later, I was still moored at the same pontoon, when this time a dead calf washed past on the current. This particular canal was starting to look like the River Styx. What next, Charon and a boat load of punters on a one way trip to the underworld?

That evening I was lamenting the emotional costs of dealing with dead and dying wildlife to Roger a new boating buddy though as I recounted the traumatic tale of the attack pigeon, I noticed that he seemed singularly underwhelmed.

"That's nothing," he explained condescendingly.

Whilst moored in La Villette the secondary port in the heart of Paris, Roger was approached by another boatie who had spotted something suspicious in the water. The two skippers wandered down the harbour wall and began prodding the sodden lump with a barge-pole only to quickly realise when the lump rolled over and stared at them through glazed unseeing eyes, that they had a genuine dead body on their hands.

Roger considered his priorities, the stiff wasn't going anywhere and he had a hard to get booking at an very exclusive restaurant in half an hours time. In a stroke of genius, Roger decided to call the police and left the other bloke holding the evidence on the end of his barge-pole until they arrived, whilst he shot through to his *dégustation* nosh up..

Later that evening when he returned, well fed from dinner, he found the port area still crammed with police cars, their blue lights were flashing and turning the port into a type of CSI playground. To make matters worse his boat was inaccessible, it had been cordoned off by yellow crime scene tape. When he approached the barrier two disheveled Maigret types stepped forward and identified themselves as undercover detectives, and insisted that by French, law the two finders would have to go to police headquarters and give a statement.

The two heroes climbed into an unmarked Gendarme-mobile of considerable antiquity, and of dubious reliability, it looked like the loser of a demolition derby. Naturally, there were with no seat belts in the rear seat, which would after all have been wasted on the criminal classes who normally were seated there and they set off towards the centre of Paris.

Five minutes later the car was stuck immobile in gridlock rush hour traffic, nothing was moving and it looked like they would be there for some hours. Maigret looked at Clouseau and said the French equivalent of, "Stuff this for a joke." Clouseau placed a blue flashing police light on the roof of the Gendarme-mobile, turned on the siren and they took off like a stabbed rat, for what was to be the most terrifying ride of Rogers life. Through red lights they rocketed, down sidewalks, through alleyways, even across a park all at breakneck speed. The old Citroën was giving its all, the tastefully placed rust holes in the exhaust, made it sound like a Formula One race car as it accelerated through gaps between parked cars that looked too small to skateboard through.

By the time he arrived at the station, Roger was a broken man and trembling like a jelly. He admitted to me later that at that point he would have signed anything put in front of him, witness statement, confession, you name it.

I had to concede that my drowning bird story was a bit lame in comparison to Rogers zombie episode but they both illustrate how life is never dull on the waterways.

By August we had at last arrived just outside of Paris and I woke up early feeling great. Inshallah, today was to be the day that we would complete the meandering journey that had lead us a merry trail across the length and breadth of France, today we would reach the centre of the most famous city in the world.

It had taken three years to get this far, at times our frustrating attempts to make any headway had felt like trying to fill the ocean with a bucket after someone on the other shore had already pulled the plug out. We were so close to our goal surely nothing could go wrong now, Paris was just around the corner?

As I stepped out of the shower, I heard the whirring of an electric motor somewhere in the bowels of the boat. What the heck was that? Any unidentified noise on a boat must be instantly located and remedied, because there are so many things that can lead to disaster if ignored. Toilets that explode, electrics catching fire, Zeppelins falling from the sky. Okay, that last one is probably not a common problem, but look what happened to the Hindenburg when coming in to port, so one can't be too careful.

There are only a few electric motors aboard, so I started by checking the usual suspects, all to no avail. Whirr..... the noise continued insistently. Next, I switched off the shore power to check that the noise was indeed of our own creation. It was. Whirr........ How could that be without any power supply?

Whirr! Perhaps the bilge pump was wired to bypass the circuit board and had cut in to handle a sudden leak. That was all we needed, sinking within sight of Paris would be the final straw. I could see tomorrows headlines in Le Figaro.

"AUSSIES SINK OUTSIDE THE PÉRIPHÉRIQUE."

Bilge pumps have a mind of their own and activate automatically when the boat is half full of water, this is not a good thing and usually implies that the bateau is about to sink unless urgent action is taken. The secondary function of the bilge pump is to give the captain a running start at abandoning ship, before women and children clog up the lifeboats. I hurriedly ripped up the floor boards to access the bilge, but there was no problem there, the bilge was dry and the pump was quiet. I was baffled.

Whirr! Still the vibrating continued unabated, there was nothing for it but to summon help. As I reached for the distress button on the VHF radio I shouted.

"Trish, see if you can find what's making that noise, before we go down with all hands."

Seconds later Trish emerged from the bathroom holding my electric razor having removed it from the shower shelf where it had lain contentedly vibrating. With a click of its button the whirring stopped and the emergency was over. With a very sheepish look, I put a hold on the Mayday calls to both the Sapeurs et Pompieurs and to CNN. I then placed the offending article back in my toilet bag banged my head a couple of times against the bulkhead and headed for a soothing coffee and a nice lie down.

By mid morning we had reached the conjuncture with the River Seine and were cruising at last through the outskirts of Paris on the most famous waterway in the world. As I stood on deck helming the mighty ship beneath me, I felt ten feet tall, like Caesar triumphantly conquering the Gauls and entering the city, Veni, Vidi, Vici, I came, saw and conquered.

213

Whack! Whack! My revelry was shattered as two eggs exploded on the deck. They were thrown by a Parisian yobbo as we passed under a bridge. This deed conclusively proved that even France has its share of people who are a slice short of a baguette.

What would Caesar have done if he had been 'egged' mid triumph? Rape the women, kill everyone and burn the town. That seemed a fair and appropriate penalty, but unable to get at the offender who loped away drunkenly, I moored alongside a péniche, cleaned the eggs off the boat, locked the doors and drank pastis until I stopped shaking. Thus fortified, the ropes were cast off again and Parce Que continued under the many bridges of Paris and into the increasingly dense commercial river traffic.

Indeed there is so much river traffic on the Seine that in the city centre there are traffic lights at the Ile de France, which change every half an hour to alternate upstream and downstream passage. As usual with traffic lights, we managed to arrive out of sync, just missing the downstream green light and so I had to dodge the upstream traffic of barges, ferries and the tourist *bateau mouches,* the long tourist cruisers, for half an hour until the signal changed. It was like playing chicken in the middle of a six lane Autobahn.

After waiting twenty minutes the lights changed and we received permission to continue. On we sailed past the majestic Notre Dame Cathedral, under the wrought iron *passerelle* walkways covered with thousands of padlocks placed on their railings as tokens of love by enamoured tourists. Make a wish, seal the padlock onto the bridge railing and throw the key away forever into the river is the idea.

Next it was past the famous Paris *Plage.* In August when the rest of France closes down for summer holidays the Paris City elders reward the millions who loyally stay in the city to keep the country running. They do this by closing down some of the roads that edge the right bank of the Seine and turn them into beachfront real estate. Truck loads of imported white sand provide the beach. Potted palm trees are freighted in, and distributed liberally for effect along the strand and there is even a shipwreck playground for the ankle-biters, there are beach volleyball courts, deck chairs and naturally there is a bar. Bands and musicians play throughout the day and Parisians take to the beach in bikinis and baste themselves with oil, desperate to get their entitlement of skin cancer and Vitamin D.

On we sailed under the magnificent Pont Alexander with its gilded statuary and its enormous central crest that looks down on the boats that have passed under it for hundreds of years. Into the very centre we motored and there on our starboard side was the magnificent Egyptian needle, its gilded spire glistening in the sun. The Luxor Obelisk is a 23 metre high monument standing at the centre of the Place de la Concorde. It was originally located at the entrance to Luxor Temple, in Egypt before Napoleon liberated it whilst ransacking the country in the name of France.

As we approached the final bend in the river the one that would lead us to the Eiffel Tower, two Police boats came hurtling towards us flashing their blue lights. What could we possibly have done? What arcane regulation had we broken? Were we to be dragged off in the aquatic paddy wagon to Police headquarters 36, Quai des Orfèvres for an enthusiastic question and answer session with some brass knuckles?

At the last moment the gendarmes veered off towards the right bank and pulled up next to a *bateau mouche*, one of the long slender glass roofed tourist boats that ply up and down the centre full of a never ending supply of wide eyed tourists. This bateau was also loaded with sightseers and for reasons unknown it had stopped in mid stream. Next thing I knew two police divers were in the water and I soon realised that they

215

were rescuing an overenthusiastic tourist who had managed to fall overboard whilst taking photographs with a selfie stick for the folks back home. She was pulled unceremoniously out of the water and wrapped in a space blanket still clinging to her dripping camera as if there would be electronic life in it after a prolonged swim in the Seine. Waving to the boys in blue, the heroes of the hour, we were on our way again.

We rounded the final bend in the river and at last there she was, the most famous erection in the world, Eiffel's tower nicknamed La Dame de Fer (The iron Lady). It was considered at the time of it's construction to be an eyesore, but now it is the most visited city landmark in the world and here we were right in front of it, at the centre of the universe. It felt great.

During the German occupation of Paris in 1940, the lift cables were cut by the French so that Adolf Hitler would have to climb the steps to the summit, thus he was denied conquering the tower and he chose to stay on the ground. Miraculously the cables were restored and the lifts were functioning within hours of the liberation of Paris. But there was to be no time for wide eyed gawping today.

"Bateau de Plaisance Parce Que, ecoutez?" "Our hand held radio crackled insistently to life next to me, shaking me out of my revelry and back into the present moment. Parisian waterway regulations state that all vessels must carry a radio open to the Paris calling frequency and all morning I had been listening uncomprehendingly to a fast flow of commercial chatter as we motored upstream, whilst deliberately keeping out of everybody's way. Now someone wanted me, but who was it and what had I possibly done?

*"Parce Que, j'ecoute '*I acknowledged. A stream of high speed Garlic blasted out of the speaker, which amazingly I understood, proving just how far our language skills had progressed since our arrival in France three years ago, when even buying a loaf of

216

bread was a linguistic Everest. The call was coming from a following vessel merely wishing to confirm that I would hold my course next to the right bank as he overtook me and not suddenly pull out in front of him and cause a collision. I confirmed my intention to comply and received a smiling courteous wave from my fellow captain as he swept past us. His boat was full of Asian tourists who pointed their expensive cameras eagerly at us and our boxing kangaroo flag, momentarily forgetting Monsieur Eiffel's large structure.

Like many people we come across, when they discover our nationality, they assume that the boat has travelled all the way from Australia. From the looks on their faces and their eager gesticulations, this lot of punters had mistaken us for mighty ocean mariners. Flat bottomed Parce Que couldn't cross anything rougher than a duck pond, let alone cross an ocean, but who was I to disillusion them and I waved back to the lens lovers with my best Captain Haddock salute?

The main port for visiting pleasure boats to Paris and our final destination was the Port de Plaisance d'Arsenal, a large marina is sunk below road level right next to the historic Place de la Bastille, the site of the beginning of the French revolution. Boats enter by a lock gate from the river and for a fraction of the cost of a Parisian hotel one can live aboard with all the comforts of home, whilst enjoying the beauty of Paris.

Arriving at the imposing gate entrance set into the right bank of the river, I called the harbourmaster on the radio and waited my turn to be locked through. Twenty minutes later it was our turn and I was just about to steer Parce Que's bows into the lock entrance, when Trish spied a large green object floating ahead. Its outline looked vaguely familiar.

"Look out! There's a bloody crocodile straight ahead, " she yelled.

"Really!" she added for emphasis and pointed just off the starboard bow.

217

You know what? She was right! This was not the sort of thing I was expecting in the heart of Paris, but it was really happening, so close to our goal and me without a 12 bore shotgun at hand. I threw the helm to port to avoid a collision and I kid you not, there was indeed a crocodile. A two metre monster of the tropics it floated smiling wickedly at us displaying a mouth full of jagged teeth, as if to deny us both entrance to the harbour and the completion of our voyage. As we came alongside, I could see it was actually only a very realistic beach toy that had blown off the nearby Paris *Plage* but it looked very convincing from a few metres away and gave us quite a turn, then it drifted past in the current to amuse other pilgrims downstream.

Into the final *écluse* of our long journey to enter the Arsenal we sailed and the lock gates closed behind us. As we ascended and entered the marina Trish and I toasted our arrival with the true Champagne from Epernay.

From Castelnaudary we had traversed France traveling thousands of kilometres at leisurely walking speed and seen so many wonderful people and places. It had taken us three years, but in spite of all the mishaps along the way or maybe even because of them we had achieved our goal and Parce Que was moored safely at last in the heart of the City of Light.

"What now?" asked Trish

"Let's just keep going." I replied. (But that's another story)

The story continues in Andrew's latest book as the voyage veers into Belgium, Germany and the Netherlands with a side trip to Tibet. Available as e-book or paperback from Amazon Books.

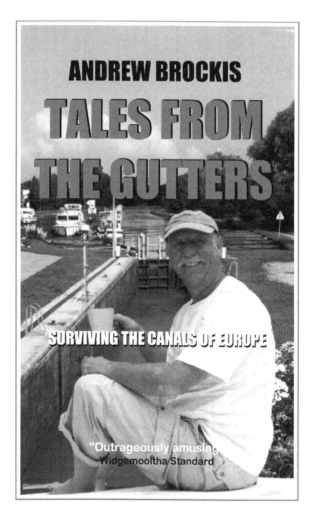

Made in the USA
Las Vegas, NV
19 November 2021

34782404R10129